ALEXFINANCENYC
PRESENTS:

BREAK UP WITH BROKE

A 5-STEP PLAN TO TRANSFORM YOUR FINANCES AND BUILD THE FUTURE YOU DESERVE

BY: ALEX TURNER & RUDI TURNER

TABLE OF CONTENTS

ACKNOWLEDGMENT

TO THE WOMEN IN MY LIFE WHO IGNITED MY PASSION AND MADE THIS BOOK POSSIBLE: BARBARA, RUDI & HARLEM

BARBARA, THANK YOU FOR LAYING THE FOUNDATION AND INSPIRING ME TO ALWAYS DO BETTER. YOU HAVE THE BIGGEST HEART OF ANYONE I KNOW, AND YOU LIT THE FIRE IN ME TO HELP PEOPLE IN NEED HOWEVER I COULD.

RUDI, THANK YOU FOR STANDING BY MY SIDE AND BRINGING OUT THE BEST IN ME. YOUR WORK ETHIC AND DRIVE ARE SECOND TO NONE, AND I'M THANKFUL THAT GOD LED ME TO YOU.

HARLEM, THANK YOU FOR PUSHING ME TO BE THE BEST VERSION OF MYSELF - SOMEONE THAT YOU CAN BE PROUD OF. GOD PUT YOU IN MY LIFE AS A CONSTANT REMINDER TO STIRVE FOR MORE AND TO TRUST THAT THE BEST IS YET TO COME.

WITHOUT YOU ALL, I WOULD NOT BE THE MAN I AM TODAY. THANK YOU.

- ALEX

PREFACE

HOW BREAKING UP WITH BROKE CHANGED MY LIFE

There comes a point when you get tired of pretending everything is fine—when the weight of credit card debt, overdraft fees, and financial anxiety becomes too heavy to hide behind a smile, and you realize the lifestyle you've been portraying to the world is just a front. That's where I was in 2015.

I wasn't only broke in terms of my bank account—I was broke in mindset, broke in habits, and broke in belief. I was working hard as a Pharmaceutical Sales Representative, but this hard work wasn't translating into any financial progress. This made my job seem even more stressful and my situation feel hopeless. Every dollar I made seemed to disappear faster than it came, and the harder I tried to "look successful," the more financially trapped I became.

Then, I realized something powerful: **being broke was a relationship *I had chosen*—and one I needed to end**. **IMMEDIATELY.** I didn't choose where I started in life, but it was up to me to determine my outcome.

That's what *Break Up With Broke* is all about. It's not just another money book. It's a wake-up call. A mindset shift. A guide for anyone ready to stop living in financial survival mode and start building a life of freedom, peace, confidence, and control.

Inside these pages, I'll walk you through the same system that helped me change my life. It helped me pay off debt, build wealth, and finally make peace with money—without giving up the things I truly love. You'll learn how to understand your habits, master your budget, prioritize what matters the most, and create a financial plan that fits your life.

Whether you're a professional making six figures but still stressed about money, a student just getting started, a couple tired of fighting over finances, or someone who simply knows they deserve a better life—this book is for you.

It's time to stop struggling in silence. It's time to stop repeating financial mistakes that don't serve you. It's time to break up with broke—***once and for all***.

Let's do it together. The journey starts now.

— Alex Turner, Founder of AlexFinanceNYC

INTRODUCTION

WHY YOU'RE HERE

Welcome, Future Millionaire! Whether you're tired of living paycheck to paycheck, want to free yourself from the never-ending cycle of debt, or simply desire more peace around your money—this guide is your first step towards breaking up with "broke" for good. With this program, you're not just learning finance fundamentals—you're building a whole new identity.

It's going to take some work, but the good news is that I have simplified the process into a 5-step method—the **5-A Way**—that will teach you how to:

- Identify and correct financial habits that are costing you money;
- Replace those habits with systems that have been proven to put more money in your pocket for the things that matter to you the most; and
- Grow your wealth in a way that makes you feel confident and secure about your financial future.

Although this isn't a "NO" plan that requires total deprivation or absolute perfection to get results, like any life changing plan, you will only get out what you put in. I know that starting your financial journey can be intimidating, overwhelming, and confusing, but the good news is, you're already well on your way to changing your financial life for good this time. You've realized that you're capable of creating better financial outcomes, have decided the time is NOW, and are committed to locking in and following a plan. If you follow this program, the only direction is up!

MEET YOUR COACH:

FORMER BROKEY TURNED MILLIONAIRE

I'm Alex: a millennial husband, father, self-made millionaire, and future multi-millionaire.

Ten years ago, I was completely broke and struggling to make ends meet due to poor spending habits and a lack of any financial knowledge. I was a twenty-something-year -old bachelor in New York City trying to find a way to balance my lifestyle and my bills. I was driving a fancy car that I couldn't afford, overwhelmed by my five-figure student loan debt, and was struggling to pay my Manhattan rent on my retail salary. I didn't know what a net worth was at that time, but let's just say mine was deep in the red.

The worst part was that I was losing hope; I had no plan and didn't know where to start. I had a Bachelor's degree in Media & Communications, but was never taught financial literacy or how to manage my money. Up to this point, I had normalized racking up debt and living check to check like everyone around me. I didn't know any millionaires, happy retirees, or anybody who was debt free. Still, somehow, I felt a sense of dissatisfaction with my situation, and I knew that I didn't want to live like this forever. One day I broke down and realized that something had to change and that I had to be the one to save me, my family, and future Alex. Let me tell you about that day and how it inspired me to break up with broke.

About a year after I had moved into my own apartment, I went back to my childhood home to visit my mother. As soon as I walked through the door, I could tell that something was wrong. The mood was somber, and my mom's energy was unusually low. My mom is a very strong and reserved person, so it took a good amount of prying for her to finally tell me what was going on. She broke down and told me that after more than thirty years of marriage – and knowing each other since they were teenagers in Antigua – my father packed up all of his belongings and left. They were getting divorced.

I felt a flood of emotions: shock, disbelief, confusion, anger, sympathy, and sadness; but most of all, I felt an overwhelming urge to rescue my mom—financially and emotionally. My father had been the breadwinner for my entire life. I had no idea how my mother would survive financially without him. She is the most generous person I know—someone who would always help a stranger in need and give her last for those she cared about. But, how would she survive and thrive on her own in this new chapter without having a financial foundation to stand on?

My parents were hard workers and always preached the importance of saving, but beyond being able to cover small emergencies, I was pretty sure my mom wasn't prepared to retire early or that there was some lofty trust fund or inheritance that would step in to replace my dad's financial contributions. Our family was far from rich, lacked financial literacy, and had no plan for anything like this. Finances weren't discussed openly in my house so I could only assume that suddenly going from a two-income household to one was going to have a serious impact.

It immediately became clear that I needed to find a way to help my mom FAST. But there was another problem: **I was beyond broke**. I'm talking living paycheck to prayer! I couldn't help myself let alone help her. This was a huge blow to my self-esteem and ego, but it was also the wake-up call that I needed. I didn't have time to feel sorry for myself. I had to figure out a way to improve my situation so that I could be a better resource for my mother.

That day my financial journey began.

After spending some time comforting my mom, I went home and got to work. First, I studied the popular finance gurus to get a basic understanding of personal finance principles. Learning about their different paths and tips motivated me, but I didn't feel like I had a clear approach that aligned with my personality and goals. Next, I web searched a ton of questions like, "How do most people get rich?", "How to save more money on a low salary?", and "What's the fastest way to become a millionaire?" Through hours and hours of research and traveling down one financial rabbit hole after another, I discovered the power of living below my means, budgeting, debt elimination, investing, and compound interest.

There was a ton of guidance available from all of these sources, but wealth building still felt overwhelming, complicated, and intimidating. I found information and inspiration, but what was missing was a clear and realistic action plan. I needed to figure out a process that was easy-to-follow and tailored to an ordinary person like me: a middle-class professional from humble beginnings who wanted to improve his financial habits, create generational wealth, and relieve financial stress and anxiety for myself and my loved ones.

I combined all of my research into a gameplan and made a promise to myself that I would lock in and follow that plan until my net worth was in the green and I no longer felt anxiety, stress, and shame every time I opened my banking app. Day by day, dollar by dollar, I slowly started budgeting, paying off my debt, saving up an emergency fund, tracking my expenses, and investing what I could.

My process definitely had some trial and error, ups and downs, and wins and losses. I had to sort out what worked from what didn't, adjust my pace at times, pivot when I hit a roadblock, and change habits and environments that were no longer serving me. Then I built momentum that became addictive. Seeing the financial growth felt amazing, but the best feeling was being able to help my mom cover her bills and pay off her own debt too.

I knew that I had found something that worked and that could help others do the same thing. I proved to myself that someone like me could build wealth without any formal financial expertise, gimmicks, or costly commitments. This is exactly the system I will teach you in this book.

Fast forward to today. I went from a net worth of ***negative $55k*** to a **$1Millon+** net worth including:

- Six-figure investment portfolio
- Six figures in home equity
- Five figures invested for my toddler's future
- Owning the luxury car of my dreams
- Zero school, auto, or consumer debt
- 800+ credit score
- Financial peace of mind

Improving my own situation also allowed me to help my mom build financial security, assist my wife with paying off her car debt and several of her student loans, and to give generously to causes that matter to me. Now, I actually look forward to checking my net worth each day and creating new financial goals for myself and my family.

I want to be clear: I missed out on some fun, sacrificed on lifestyle splurges, dealt with nay-sayers, and had to constantly motivate myself while taking this road less travelled; but, that one decision to stick with a plan to prioritize my finances over my lifestyle changed my life in ways I never dreamed possible. The same can happen for you. If anything in my story resonates with you, then you have come to the right place. I have combined all of my knowledge, personal lessons, and tips into the **5-A Way** that I have used to help dozens of clients achieve their financial goals and transform their lives.

The habits and techniques that you will learn in this step-by-step guide are the same principles that I applied to become a millionaire in just nine years while working a 9-5 and without any special inheritance or formal financial education. If I can do it, you can do it too! All you need is a plan - which you are holding in your hands as we speak- and consistency. Starting this program is a great first step towards breaking up with broke forever and ensuring your financial success. Let's break up with broke together!

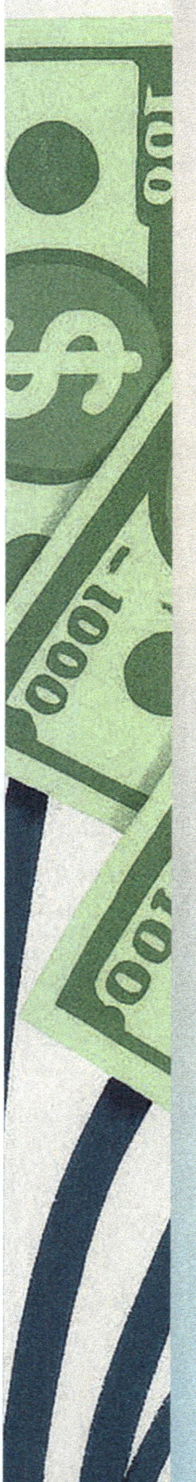

CHAPTER 1

GET YOUR MIND RIGHT: FINANCIAL IDENTITY RESET

Step 1:
Before your bank account can change, your mindset must change.

Mastering your money starts with unlearning the myths that have kept you stuck—like the idea that debt is normal, that budgeting means deprivation, or that wealth is only for the lucky. If you're tired of the stress, the juggling, the uncertainty, the constant paycheck-to-paycheck cycle, then it's time for a mindset reset.

This chapter is your wake-up call. If nothing changes, the risk is real: foreclosure, repossession, poor credit, bankruptcy, poverty, financial desperation, and the mental toll that comes with it. The good news? You have the power to shift your situation. By living on less than you make, prioritizing your goals, and committing to a step-by-step plan, you can raise your net worth, grow your savings, improve your credit score, and finally feel free—even richer—without debt payments draining your future. This is where the journey begins: not just to financial freedom, but to peace, confidence, and wealth that lasts.

**MONEY MYTHS KEEP YOU BROKE.
LET'S BREAK THEM.**

Common Myths:

- "I'm just bad with money."
- "Debt is normal."
- "I'll save when I earn more."

Truths to Replace Them:

- Good money management is a skill, not a personality trait.
- I don't need debt to achieve my financial milestones or acquire assets.
- Even small amounts saved consistently will add up over time.

By focusing on what you can do rather than what you lack, you can cultivate gratitude and create more positive financial experiences. Also, we know the power of the mind is a real thing, so believing you can win with money is key to bringing your financial goals to fruition.

Step 2: Exposing Limiting Beliefs

A limiting belief is a thought or conviction you accept as truth, often held unconsciously, that restricts your potential, ability to achieve your goals, and embrace new opportunities. These beliefs, which may be based on past experiences, fears, or societal expectations, can act as barriers to your growth and success.

Uncovering limiting beliefs is one of the most important steps in building wealth – because your mindset drives your money habits. If you don't reprogram your thoughts around money, you'll keep sabotaging your progress, even with a solid budget or financial plan. It's important to think about where these beliefs stem from so that you can break them. Ask yourself these questions to better understand how your mindset impacts your relationship with money:

1) How does money make you feel (anxious, stressed, excited, proud)?

2) Where did you learn about money?

3) Did your money lessons come from someone who was financially secure?

4) Do you talk about money with anyone in your circle? If so, how often? are these deep conversations or surface level? are these conversations negative and confrontational or are they encouraging and insightful? If you don't talk about money with your circle, why not?

5) What kind of relationship did you have with money growing up? How has that shaped how you handle money as an adult?

In Step 1, we identified some examples of money myths. Now let's think about why we have become so conditioned to believing them.

- **Beliefs:** What are some limiting beliefs that you have about money and finances?
- **Origin:** What is the source (who told you that/where does that belief come from)?
- **Reflection:** Has that belief helped or hurt you financially? What if the opposite were true?
- **Truth**: How can we reframe a limiting belief into a truth statement that empowers us on our financial journey.

Examples:

Belief	Origin	Truth Replacement
I will always be in debt	I watched my parents struggle with debt.	I can change my story and become the lender instead of the borrower.
I'm not good with money	I never learned about managing money at home or in school.	I'm learning how to manage money with confidence and clarity.
Talking about money is impolite/ taboo/ will cause a fight	My family never talked about money except when arguing.	Talking about money strengthens relationships, normalizes financial goals and struggles, and fosters support.
People like me can't be rich	Most of my friends and family are drowning in debt or living check to check.	I can be a wealth success story.
I don't deserve to be wealthy	I was taught that wanting more is greedy or selfish.	Wealth allows me to help others and live in alignment with my values.

Use this Limiting Beliefs Worksheet to reflect on your own limiting beliefs about money:

Belief	Origin	Truth Replacement

Step 3: Set Financial Intentions

Now that we have identified some of the money myths and limiting beliefs that may be stunting our financial growth, it's time to make an action plan. People are more likely to shift their mindset when they can see how the new belief applies to them.

Start by answering these questions:

- What does financial freedom look like for me?
- How do I want to feel about money?
- What's one thing I'll stop doing and one thing I'll start doing to make financial freedom a reality?

Success Tip: Write 3 money affirmations and put them where you'll see them daily. People need to hear new truths more than once to override old beliefs, so make it a daily habit to read them out loud with conviction. Repetition and reinforcement are essential to shifting your mindset and preparing you for financial abundance. If you need some inspiration, I got you:

You's a paper chaser. You got your budget on fire. Investing and saving. Until the moment you retire. You handle your biz. No more moving off desire. You breaking up with broke. So your wealth can climb higher!

💌 ***Letter to My Future Self***

Keep this as a reminder for the days you feel stuck, overwhelmed, or unsure. This is your proof that you made a decision to change your story—and that you're already becoming who you were meant to be.

Date: ___________________________

Dear Future Me,

I'm writing this letter from the beginning of something powerful. Today, I decided to break up with broke—not just in my bank account, but in my mindset, in my habits, and in the way I see myself. I may not have it all figured out just yet, but I know this: I'm no longer living on autopilot or making excuses for being stuck.

I've taken steps to:

- Face my finances with honesty
- Create systems that support me
- Set goals that reflect my values
- Build a future that feels free, not fearful

You've come a long way since the day I picked up this guide. I hope you've stayed consistent, even when it was hard. I hope you've remembered your why, even when it felt far away. I hope you've given yourself grace when things didn't go as planned. And I hope you're proud—not just of your progress, but of your persistence.

💌 *Letter to My Future Self (continued)*

Here's what I want you to never forget:

- You are not defined by your debt.
- You are worthy of abundance, peace, and joy.
- You can always start again, smarter and stronger.
- And you never have to be broke—mentally, emotionally, or financially—ever again.

When you read this in the future, I hope you smile. I hope you remember how far you've come. And I hope you thank the version of yourself who made this choice—to build, to believe, and to break free.

Keep going. Keep growing.

The best is still ahead.

With pride and power,

____

Your Day-One Self 💪

Step 4: Create an Environment Where You Can Succeed

When accountability is built into your environment, progress becomes sustainable, setbacks feel less isolating, and success feels far more achievable. A financial accountability partner is someone who helps you stay consistent and honest about your money goals — kind of like a gym buddy, but for your finances.

Here's an easy way to think about it: They're the person you check in with regularly to review your spending, savings, and goals — making sure you actually do what you said you'd do with your money.
A good accountability partner:

- Keeps you on track when you're tempted to overspend.
- Celebrates wins like paying off debt or hitting a savings goal.
- Pushes you to stay disciplined and make better financial decisions.

In short: they help turn good intentions into real financial progress. When I defined my financial goals, I knew my lifestyle would have to change dramatically. One of the first steps was creating an environment that would support those goals. Here's how I did it:

First, I texted my mom and asked to talk

face-to-face. I went to her house and explained that I was in a bad place financially. I showed her my phone: my checking account was overdrawn, I had about $20,000 in credit card debt, and I owed roughly $30,000 in student loans.

I knew I had to get out of debt to make the progress I believed I could make. I had already calculated that it would take about two-and-a-half years if I was aggressive. During that conversation, I told my mom that to make real progress, I would need to be *very* disciplined with my money for a while. That meant that our tradition of expensive gifts for every holiday would be suspended for a while. It was a hard conversation—most people are short-sighted, and that amount of time can feel like a decade—but my mom saw the vision and was nothing but supportive. She told me to take all the time I needed to get myself together, not to worry about her, and reminded me that celebration isn't measured by what you buy.

Next, it was time to sit down with the people I had spent the most time and money with over the past ten years—my "Bros." I sent a message in our group chat calling a meeting at my house. As they arrived one by one, I second-guessed whether I had the courage to be fully transparent with them. I was embarrassed and afraid they would judge me. Aside from my mom, I had never talked to anyone about my finances. I tried to start the conversation by asking for their help, but it was hard for me to find the right words. So, I opened my phone and showed them exactly what was going on with my finances and let the numbers do the talking. I told them my first mission was to get completely out of debt as fast as possible. In order to devote as much of my income as possible to that goal, I couldn't keep traveling, clubbing, brunching, or shopping with them. I told them to call me out if they saw me spending on anything that didn't support my goal. I still wanted to spend time together, but we would need to find new ways that didn't cost hundreds of dollars for every outing. I suggested more game nights, playing basketball, or finding free events as a start.

The reactions were mixed. Two of them thought I was out of my mind for taking such an extreme approach to a common issue. Still, they said they would respect my decision. Two others were fully supportive and did not have strong opinions one way or the other. The last two, who shared they were also silently fighting the same battles, were enthusiastic about my new journey and motivated to also try making changes of their own. After those conversations, my mind was clear, I felt relieved, and I was ready to attack my goals.

My advice to you is to tell people about your journey as soon as possible so that you can find support and accountability or, if necessary, prepare to create boundaries where there may be obstacles.

Once you've shared your goals with a financial accountability partner, the next step is shaping your surroundings to make success easier and temptation harder. That might mean deleting tempting apps, unsubscribing from promotional emails, and unfollowing social media accounts that encourage impulse spending, and removing saved credit cards from shopping apps or your digital wallet. These small, intentional changes reduce daily temptation around spending and help your environment work for your goals instead of against them.

If you don't have a financial accountability partner nearby, don't panic. You can always reach out to me personally at alexfinancenyc@gmail.com or join the alexfinancenyc community (check out alexfinancenyc.com for more details).

Your mindset is your financial foundation. In Chapter 1, you confronted the thoughts, fears, and financial habits that have kept you stuck. We explored how your money mindset was shaped by family, culture, or past experiences and you learned how to rewrite those narratives, so they work *for* you instead of against you. By reframing how you think about money you'll build the clarity and confidence you need to take control of your finances and your future.

If you ever feel stuck, come back to these steps:

Before your bank account can change, your mindset must change

Exposing Limiting Beliefs Allows You to Rewrite Them

Setting Financial Intentions Helps You Align Your Money With Your Values

Create an Environment Where You Can Succeed

CHAPTER 2

BREAKING UP WITH BROKE THE "5-A WAY"

Now that we have a clean mental slate, it's time to really dig in.

In this chapter we will be using my five-step process to build a financial plan that will allow you to track and regulate your spending (*budgeting) while increasing your net worth by reducing your debt. It's called:

THE

5-A WAY

1. ANALYZE
2. ACKNOWLEDGE
3. ATTACK
4. ADJUST
5. APPLAUD

If you've ever felt like your paycheck disappears before you can even enjoy it, or like your debt is silently stealing your freedom, you're not alone. Debt can feel heavy, overwhelming, and even shameful—but it doesn't have to define you. In this chapter, we're not just talking about numbers—we're talking about taking your power back. Whether it's credit cards, student loans, or that car note you regret, this is your blueprint to break up with debt once and for all. Step by step, you'll use the **5-A Way** to build a plan that fits your life, keeps you motivated, and helps you move from stressed to unstoppable. Let's clear the clutter, reclaim your cash flow, and start walking toward the financial freedom you deserve.

Step 1: Analyze Your Numbers

SECTION 1: YOUR WEALTH SCOREBOARD

Before you can break up with broke, you need to understand where you stand. Think of your finances like school—except instead of getting grades in science or English, you're getting a score in money management. Your financial report card tells the story of your money habits, strengths, and areas that need some love. This chapter will help you decode that report card, so you can stop guessing and start making power moves.

What Is a Financial Report Card?

Just like in school, your financial report card is made up of multiple scores and indicators that evaluate how you are progressing and where you are performing in relation to expected targets you should be meeting. No single number defines your financial health—it's a combo of stats that show how you're managing your money. Let's break down the most important ones:

Your Net Worth: The Big Picture 

Your net worth is your financial GPA. It's the clearest snapshot of your overall financial standing. You calculate it by subtracting your liabilities from your assets: **Net Worth = Assets – Liabilities**

- ***Assets***: What you **own**. This includes things like cash, your checking account balance, investments, car equity, home equity, and retirement accounts.
- ***Liabilities***: What you **owe**. Think Buy Now, Pay Later, credit card balances, car loans, student loans, mortgages, personal loans, and any other debts.

Let's walk through an example together:

If you have
- $5,000 in savings;
- $10,000 in your 401k; and
- a $12,000 car that's fully paid off

your assets = **$27,000** ($5,000 + $10,000 + $12,000).

if you owe:
- $1,000 in credit card debt;
- $12,000 in student loans; and
- have no money saved

your liabilities = **$13,000** ($1,000 +$12,000).

Your net worth is your assets (**$27,000**) – your liabilities (**$13,000**) = **$14,000**

Take a moment to calculate your net worth. If this number is positive, Congrats! You're already off to a strong start. If it's negative, don't panic! A negative net worth doesn't mean failure; it means you have a baseline to grow from. What truly matters is knowing where you started because that starting point gives meaning to every step forward. Financial confidence is built by understanding your reality and proving to yourself that you're moving in the right direction one decision at a time.

As you implement the strategies from each chapter, your net worth will be how we track the progress. When you track your numbers, you can see progress that most people miss: debt shrinking, savings growing, and habits improving.

Your Credit Score: The Trust Factor

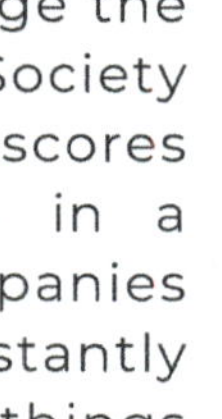

Your credit score is like a trust meter for lenders. It shows how well you manage the money you owe other people. Society places a lot of weight on credit scores because – let's face it – we live in a consumer-driven culture where companies thrive off of getting people to constantly spend money they don't have on things they don't need. Strong credit can be a useful tool – we'll talk more about this in Chapter 6– but it is by no means the end all be all or the best indicator of your wealth or financial health.

Score ranges:

- 800–850: Excellent
- 740–799: Very Good
- 670–739: Good
- 580–669: Fair
- Below 580: Poor

According to data from a top credit bureau, the average credit score in 2025 was 715. You should aim to have and maintain at least “very good” credit at all times.

What impacts your score?

- **Payment history** – Do you pay on time? (most important)

- **Credit utilization** – How much of your available credit you’re using (aim for under 10%)

- **Length of credit history** – Older accounts show long-term, responsible use of credit.

- **Credit mix** – A variety of account types (credit cards, auto loans, student loans, mortgages) shows that you are capable of handling different types of credit responsibly.

- **New credit** – Too many new accounts could be a red flag that you’re gearing up to take on too much debt and might struggle to repay it.

Pro Tip: Check your credit score regularly (The Internet offers free tools). Maintaining a strong credit score helps you qualify for lower interest rates on a home, and even some jobs or apartments.

Other Key Indicators of Financial Health

1. Savings Rate: *What percentage of your income are you saving?*

If you're saving at least 20% of your income, you're doing well. But if you're starting at 5%, that's okay too—as long as you're consistent and increasing when you can.

2. Debt-to-Income (DTI) Ratio: How much of your monthly income goes toward debt payments?

DTI = Monthly debt payments ÷ Monthly income

This number helps lenders decide if you can handle more credit. Keep it under 36% for good financial health (lower is better and 0% is ideal!)

3. Emergency Fund: Do you have at least 6 months of all your expenses saved?

This fund keeps you from falling into debt when life starts "life-ing"—like job loss, car repairs, or unexpected bills. Six months is a solid goal, but keep in mind that this amount may need to be higher depending on whether/how many other people depend on you, the type of work you do (I'm looking at you, gig workers and freelancers!), the state of the world, or other factors. Here's what a good cushion looks like for these 3 scenarios:

Single

- **Goal**: 6 months of your essential expenses
- **Focus**: Job loss, medical bills, car repairs

Couple (No Kids)

- **Goal**: 6-9 months of household expenses
- **Focus**: same as above + shared bills

Family (With Kids)/Single Parents

- **Goal**: 9–12 months of family expenses
- **Focus**: same as above + childcare, unexpected kid expenses
- **Tip**: Bigger cushion = less stress — this is for protection, not growth

Bottom line:
The more people relying on your income, the larger your emergency fund must be.

I have been let go from jobs at times when I did and did not have an emergency fund set to the side. When I didn't have enough tucked away, I felt anxious, stressed, and powerless. When I had money set to the side and was faced with job loss, I felt prepared, proud, and at peace. Ask yourself which position you would rather be in.

4. *Spending Habits*: Are you spending intentionally or impulsively?

Tracking your spending (even for 30 days) can reveal patterns. You might discover subscriptions you forgot about or spending leaks that are holding you back (such as lifestyle creep and impulse spending).

Lifestyle creep—when your spending quietly increases as your income goes up—may also be silently draining your progress. Picture this: You get a raise, but instead of saving or investing the extra, you start upgrading your lifestyle —nicer apartment, more takeout, newer car, luxury vacations —and before you know it, your paycheck still disappears just as fast as before. In short, your lifestyle "creeps up" to match your income, leaving you no better off financially despite earning more money.

Throw undisciplined budgeting, pressure to keep up with the Joneses, and poor financial habits in the mix and you have a recipe for disaster. What you should do instead: when your income increases, pay your future self first (by investing and saving a portion) before adjusting your lifestyle. It's okay to treat yourself and celebrate but limiting lifestyle creep ensures your spending remains aligned with your values and long-term goals. You'll progress faster this way too.

5. Income Growth
Are you increasing your income over time? Whether it's negotiating raises and

promotions, picking up a side hustle, or investing in your skills, income growth is a major sign of financial momentum.

 ***Why This Matters***

Think of this chapter as your financial "check engine" light. You don't have to fix everything at once—but you do have to pop the hood and look inside regularly. Understanding your net worth, credit score, and other indicators gives you a baseline. From here, you can set goals, track progress, and make your money start working for you.

Just like cars require regular maintenance and report cards track quarterly progress, you need to review your financial report card on a regular basis. I review mine every day—not because there are drastic changes —but because I have made it a habit to know my numbers, and the constant reminder of my progress motivates me to keep going hard!

Sometimes my net worth goes down temporarily—like when the stock market takes a dip or an emergency requires me to dip into my emergency fund—but over time, I have watched this number steadily grow from negative **$55k** to over **$1M**.

Remember, you're not being graded—you're gaining insight. This is your chance to be the CFO of your life. And trust me: the more you know, the more you'll grow.

Snapshot of Your Financial Health

Now that you know what your net worth, credit score, and emergency fund are, the next step is simple—but powerful: write them down. Putting the numbers on paper turns vague awareness into real clarity. You can't improve what you don't measure, and this is where progress actually starts—by facing the numbers and giving yourself a clear starting point to build from. Use honest grades based on how you feel about each area. It's not about judgment—it's about clarity.

Indicator	My Number / Notes	Grade (A–F)	Notes for Improvement
Net Worth	$__________	___	______________________________
Credit Score	__________	___	______________________________
Emergency Fund	$__________	___	______________________________
Debt Balance	$__________	___	______________________________
Debt-to-Income Ratio	________%	___	______________________________
Monthly Savings Rate	________%	___	______________________________
Spending Habits	(Intentional? Impulsive?)	___	______________________________
Income Growth	(Stable? Growing?)	___	______________________________

Pro Tip: A positive net worth is a great goal, but don't stress if it's negative right now—especially if you're just getting started. Knowing your number is the most important part. Knowing helps you build and the positive habits and systems we put in place now will ensure consistent growth for the future.

My Financial Strengths: *What am I doing well right now?*

1.
2.
3.
4.
5.

<u>SMART Goals Based on My Report Card</u> 

Write 1–2 clear, actionable goals based on what your report card reveals.

Goal 1:

(Example: "Build a $1,000 emergency fund in 3 months by saving $85/week.")

Goal 2:

(Example: "Lower my credit utilization to 10% or less by paying $200 extra per month on my credit card.")

✨ Reflect
"I am not defined by this report card—I am empowered by it."

How do I feel after completing this?

Want to know how you're stacking up against your peers?

Age of head of family	Median net worth	Average net worth
Under 35	$39,040.	$183,380.
35-44	$135,300.	$548,070.
45-54	$246,700.	$971,270.
55-64	$364,270.	$1,564,070.
65-74	$410,000.	$1,780,720.
75+	$334,700.	$1,620,100.

This data is from the Survey of Consumer Finances. The Federal Reserve Board issues the survey every three years to share information about family incomes, net worth, retirement savings and more. The most recent report was released in October 2023.

Step 2: Budgeting-You Can't Fix What You Don't Track

Most people stay broke not because they don't make enough, but because they're clueless about how their money moves. You may think you have it under control or "it's not that bad," but the cold, hard truth is that ***what isn't measured, isn't managed*** (say it one more time for the people in the back!). The numbers don't lie! They tell an accurate and unbiased story about what your priorities are. This section will show you how to shine a light on your finances so you can stop guessing, start planning, and build a foundation for real, lasting wealth.

Tracking your finances is the first step to taking control of your financial future. It's not just about budgeting – it's about building awareness. Regularly reviewing your spending is essential because awareness is the foundation of financial change. Without regularly reviewing where your money is going, it's easy to slip back into old habits, overspend in certain areas or miss opportunities to save or invest. When you know exactly how much you earn, spend, and save, you will expose hidden habits, uncover waste, and create space for intentional progress.

Budgeting without guilt
Budgeting should reflect your values, not your restrictions. A budget is a living tool, not a one-time event.

Use a Needs based Budgeting Framework – *The Waterfall Rule*

"The Waterfall Rule" in budgeting means you give every dollar a job by "flowing" your income down through categories in strict priority order, like water cascading down steps: Needs → Savings → Wants.

- *Needs*: Essentials that must be covered before anything else: housing, utilities, food, and transportation.
- *Savings*: This bucket is where you pay yourself first. It's designed to capture a portion of your income for future goals, emergencies, and financial security.

Examples: an emergency fund (minimum of $1000) or sinking funds for upcoming *mandatory* expenses (medical procedure, car maintenance, etc.). Next comes debt payments starting with minimum balances and then shoveling any extra money toward the highest-priority balance. Once the savings are secure and debt is gone, the next layer is investing for long-term wealth building.

- *Wants*: This bucket covers the things that add enjoyment to your life—concerts, shopping, vacation, dining out or entertainment. It's where you intentionally budget for the things you love, guilt-free, after your needs and savings are handled. Enjoy yourself!

Your waterfall budget works best when every dollar has a purpose. By letting your income "flow" through each bucket—needs, savings, and wants—you create a system that balances responsibility with freedom. This approach ensures your essentials are covered, your future is funded, and you still have room to enjoy life today. Remember: it's not about restriction - it's about direction.

Use this Monthly Spending Snapshot Template to start your Waterfall Budget:

Month: ______________________________

Total Monthly Income: _______________

Needs:

Category	Amount Spent	Notes
Housing		
Transportation		
Insurance		
Phone Bill		
Internet		
Childcare		
Tuition		
Debt (**see* Debt Inventory Template below)		
Groceries		
Total:		

Savings

Category	Amount Spent	Notes
Emergency Fund		
Retirement		
Investments		
Extra debt payments		
Other savings goals		
Miscellaneous		
Total:		

Wants:

Category	Amount Spent	Notes
Travel		
Eating Out		
Shopping		
Entertainment		
Personal Care		
Miscellaneous		
Total:		

Use this Debt Inventory Template to get clear on what you owe and who you owe. You'll need to:

- Collect statements or log into accounts.
- Complete the worksheet below.
- **Don't skip anything**: credit cards, student loans, personal loans, car notes, mortgage, medical loans, IRS, payday loans, buy now, pay later, the $40 you borrowed from your homegirl, etc.

Creditor	Type (credit card, loan, etc.)	Amount	Interest Rate	Minimum Monthly Payment	Due Date
Store Card #1	Credit Card	$3,200	22%	$95	15th

Summary

Category	Amount	Notes
Total income		
Needs Total		
Savings Total		
Wants Total		

Your income **must** be greater than your expenses for this plan to work. If your expenses are higher than your income, you have to:

Cut expenses (start with wants, then explore your options around your biggest, fixed costs like housing or your car)
Increase income (a new job/career, overtime, side hustles, selling unused items, or negotiating pay are great options)

I suggest utilizing both for maximum results.

<u>Review Monthly & Adjust</u>
Your snapshot acts like a financial mirror: it shows you what's working, what's not, and where your money habits need a reset. By reviewing it at least monthly, you can track your progress, stay aligned with your goals, and make intentional adjustments before small leaks turn into big problems. It's not about tracking for tracking's sake – it's about using that information to make smarter, more intentional money moves each month.

Step-by-step Budget Guide (use this every month)

1) <u>Map your month & income</u>

- Write down the dates and net (a.k.a. "take home pay") amounts of your paychecks for the month (For example, "Paycheck 1- November 15 ($4,000)" and "Paycheck 2- November 30 ($4,000)").

2) Make a paycheck calendar

- Match each bill to the paycheck that comes before its due date.

- Under paycheck 1, list every bill (and its due date) that is due between the 15th and 29th. Under paycheck 2, list every bill that is due from the 1st to the 14th. Every one of your bills should appear under one of these two checks.

- Decide your focus for the month (e.g., "finish $500 for emergency fund" or "attack credit card #1").

- If you need to, split variable costs (groceries, gas, personal care, etc.) across both checks so you don't run dry mid-month.

3) Allocate in strict order (waterfall rule)

A. *Needs (must-pay essentials first)*

- Housing, utilities, groceries, transportation, insurance, childcare, phone/internet.

- Cover the full month of needs across your two checks before anything else.

B. *Debt (minimums first, then extra to the target debt)*

- Pay all minimums across debts.

- Put every extra dollar this month on the single highest-priority debt.

C. *Savings (cash)*

- Build/maintain your Emergency Fund (target at least $1,000 starter → then 6 months after paying debt (or more, *see* p. 26, depending on the size of your family).
- Add sinking funds (car maintenance, annual bills) so irregular expenses don't blow up your budget.

D. *Investing (post-tax)*

- Fund Roth IRA/brokerage from take-home pay.
- If you also contribute to a 401(k) through payroll, that happens pre-tax—great!—but still plan your post-tax investing here.

E. Wants *(last on purpose)*

- Dining out, subscriptions, entertainment, personal spending. Only fund Wants after A–D are satisfied.

4) <u>*Use target ranges (adjust to your situation)*</u>

- **Needs**: Ideally ~50% of net pay (lower this as much as possible by downgrading living situation, house-hacking or sharing costs) this gap is where wealth is built over time
- **Debt**: (include minimum payments + extra): 10–20% (be as aggressive as you can be)
- **Savings**: 5–10% (more if you are working on building your emergency fund)
- **Investing** (post-tax): 10–15% (on top of any payroll 401(k))

- Wants: 5–10% (flex bucket that expands/shrinks based on your goals)

5) *Use a Zero-based budget for each paycheck*

- For each paycheck, assign EVERY dollar a job until the "Unassigned" amount is $0.
- If anything remains, throw it towards your smallest debt (or Emergency Fund if that's your #1 goal).

6) *Track actuals weekly*

- Mid-month: compare your budgeted numbers vs. your actual spend, adjust the second paycheck's plan, and protect your top priority.
- End-month: roll any positive leftover to debt or savings—not wants.

7) *Rinse & Improve*

- If Needs > 60%: cut or renegotiate expenses (housing, insurance, cell, internet, etc.), cut back on "wants," consider side income, new job or higher paying career)

When your emergency fund is complete and your high-interest debt is gone, shift all extra money to investing.

Budget example (numbers you can mimic)

Assume your net income is $8,000 this month ($4,000 per paycheck).

Paycheck 1 $4000 (covers early bills & variable costs):

- Needs: Groceries $600, Electricity $100, Cell Phone $100, Gas $50, Laundry $20, Hair Care $50, Transit $150 → $1,070

- Debt: Capital One Credit Card $1500, Old Navy Credit Card $200, Macy's Credit Card $180 → $1,880

- Savings: Emergency Fund $850

- Wants: Entertainment $200

Paycheck 2 $4000 (covers later bills + goals):

- Needs: Rent $3000, Groceries $600 → $3600

- Save: $300

- Wants: Entertainment $100

Pay Date: 4/15	Pay Amount: $ 4,000.00	
Expense	Expense Amount	Due Date
Groceries	($600.00)	n/a
Electricity	($100.00)	4/17
Cell Phone	($100.00)	4/19
Home Gas	($50.00)	4/18
Laundry	($20.00)	n/a
Hair Care	($50.00)	n/a
Transit	($150.00)	n/a
Save	($850.00)	n/a
Bank Credit Card	($1,500.00)	4/19
Store Credit Card #1	($200.00)	4/20
Store Credit Card #2	($180.00)	4/20
Entertainment	($200.00)	n/a
Pay Date: 4/31	Pay Amount: $ 4,000.00	
Expense	Expense Amount	Due Date
Rent	($3,000)	5/1
Groceries	($600)	n/a
Save	($300.00)	n/a
Entertainment	($100)	n/a

Saving on Essentials

Mastering the cost of your essentials is the foundation of real financial change. This may feel small, but these decisions compound faster than almost anything else. Groceries, housing, utilities, insurance, and transportation quietly shape your entire financial picture. Learning how to optimize these areas gives you immediate wins that build momentum, making long-term goals feel achievable instead of overwhelming.

When you consistently live below your means, the benefits compound far beyond money. You reduce financial pressure, improve decision-making, and give yourself margin in every area of life. That margin is what allows you to stay calm during setbacks, avoid unnecessary debt, and keep progressing even when income fluctuates. In the long run, this stability becomes one of your greatest assets.

Some of my earliest wins came from the very tips and hacks I'm about to share with you. The combination of cutting subscriptions, cable TV, using unemployment benefits, house hacking, selecting a cheaper cell phone plan, cutting out takeout, and selling my car changed my life and made me feel like I had enough money to hit all of my wealth building goals.

This next section breaks down dozens of tried-and-true tips and hacks to reduce your expenses to free up more income for saving, investing, and the things that matter to you.

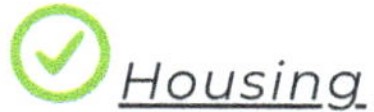

Housing

1. Move back home (if possible):
    - Share your plan with your parents and offer to contribute a reasonable amount to household expenses. They will be great accountability partners, and this arrangement can fast-track you to your financial goals.
2. Negotiate your rent or mortgage:
    - *Renters*: Ask for a rent reduction in exchange for a longer lease, prepaying a few months, or agreeing to handle minor maintenance.
    - *Homeowners*: Refinance when interest rates drop, or look into first-time homeowner or community programs that reduce property taxes.

2. Downsize or Right-Size:
    - Are you paying for unused space? In high-cost cities, even 100–200 sq. ft. less can save hundreds per month. Consider whether you can move to a smaller apartment or home that still fits your needs.

3. House Hack
    - Rent out a spare room, basement, garage, or parking spot.
    - Take on a roommate and split utilities, rent, internet, groceries etc.
    - Use your home as a short-term rental if allowed.

4. Relocate Strategically
    - Moving just outside a high-demand area (15–20 minutes from a city center) can cut costs by 20–40%.
    - Look for emerging neighborhoods that are less popular, undervalued, or have more competitive rents
5. Use Employer & Government Programs
    - Check if your employer offers relocation or housing stipends
    - Look into housing assistance programs (first-time buyer credits, down payment assistance, Section 8)
    - Some cities offer rent control or income-based housing options.
6. Reduce Utility & Maintenance Costs
    - Ask landlord to cover utilities in exchange for committing to a longer lease. If you are a good tenant who pays on time, they might agree for no extra cost or commitment.
    - For homeowners: keep up with preventative maintenance (roof, HVAC, plumbing) to avoid expensive emergency repairs.
    - Consider energy-efficient upgrades—many local governments provide rebates for insulation, efficient windows, or solar panels.

7. Creative Alternatives

- Co-living spaces: private bedrooms with shared kitchens are often cheaper than solo renting.
- Live-in opportunities: caretaking or property manager roles may provide discounted or free housing. (live-in super, dorm resident assistant, Airbnb property manager, live-in caretaker for elderly patients, etc.)
- Tiny homes/accessory dwelling units can be cheaper to own or rent.

 *Utilities*

- *Electricity*: Switch to LED bulbs, set the thermostat 2–3° lower/ higher,, and unplug "energy vampires" (devices and appliances that consume electricity even when they are not in use, like chargers, game consoles, and printers).
- *Water*: Fix leaks, install low-flow showerheads, and have a shower time limit.
- *Internet/Phone*: Bundle services, negotiate with providers for a "customer loyalty discount," or switch to smaller carriers for 50–70% savings.

- Compare providers: Call annually—loyalty often costs more than switching. There is always a competitor who would be glad to have your business.

Food & Groceries

1. Meal Planning & Cooking at Home
   - Repeat after me: YOU DO NOT HAVE FAST FOOD MONEY. On average, it's about **five times** more expensive to order food from a delivery app than cooking at home. That money can add up quickly!
   - Plan meals weekly around what's on sale—this avoids impulse buys.
   - Batch cooking/freezing: Set aside leftover portions for future meals to avoid food waste and expensive last-minute takeout.
2. Grocery Shopping Hacks
   - Buy in bulk: Warehouse Wholesale clubs offer great value for families or roommates who can split bulk buys for the items you use the most.
   - Discount grocers are consistently cheaper for basics that are still high quality.
   - Unit pricing matters: Check cost per ounce/lb instead of package price.

3. Timing and Where You Shop

    - Shop weekly, not daily. Fewer trips = fewer temptations.
    - Discount days: Some stores offer senior, student, or military discounts on specific days.
    - Check for store coupons and weekly promotions.
    - Farmers markets: vendors often discount items at the end of the day to clear stock.

4. Cut Convenience & Waste

    - Skip pre-cut produce & prepackaged snacks, which can be marked up 3–5x.
    - Freeze extras before they spoil.
    - Get creative with leftovers: turn near-expired veggies into stir-fry or soup.
    - Use "ugly produce" boxes: services online offer 25–50% savings on food that doesn't meet store standards for aesthetics (like oddly shaped or sized apples) but is otherwise perfectly fine in terms of quality and taste.

5. Dining Out Smarter

    - Bring your lunch: A $12 work lunch daily=~$3,000/year. If you're 25, investing that amount could grow to about $45k that you could use in retirement to travel the world or buy a brand new coupe CASH.

- Set a cap on 1-2 meals out per month.
- If you are eating out, happy hour and lunch specials can be cheaper than dinner menus.
- Clarify at the beginning of a group outing whether the bill will be split or not. Don't be ashamed to ask for your own check so that you can control your budget.
- Share entrées or skip drinks/dessert, which are often the biggest markup items.
- Download an app that connects customers with restaurants, bakeries, and grocery stores that sell surplus food at the end of the day for a steep discount—typically at 50–70% off regular prices—helping users save money while reducing food waste.

6. Extra Savings Tools

- Cashback apps offer cash back rewards for everyday spending on items like groceries and household items

Transportation

- Is a car ***essential*** for you to get to

work? Do you ***need*** a car for any other reason (i.e., take kids to school) Can you walk, bike, carpool or use public transportation instead?

- Do you have ***too much car***? Can you downsize/ change brands/ get an older model to cut your car note?
- Combine errands, avoid rush hour, and keep tires inflated to save on gas, parking, and tolls.
- Check if your employer offers pre- tax savings for transportation costs like public transportation and parking.
- Public transit passes: Monthly or annual passes are often cheaper than daily fares.
- Maintenance: Regular oil changes & tire rotations prevent costly breakdowns.
- Rideshare hacks: If needed, try carpool options from rideshare apps.

Insurance (Health, Car, Home, etc.)

- Compare at least 3-4 providers every renewal cycle. Consider some of the less-known/popular options - just because they spend less on advertising doesn't mean they offer inferior coverage.
- Bundling different types of insurance (i.e., home + auto) can save hundreds

- Increase deductibles: If you have an emergency fund, raising deductibles can slash premiums.
- Drop extras: Cancel overlapping coverage (e.g., roadside assistance if you already have AAA).
- Short-Term ("Term") vs. Whole Life Insurance: Term life insurance is like renting coverage for a set period — like 10, 20, or 30 years —that only pays out if you pass away during that time. Whole life insurance is more expensive but lasts your entire life and builds cash value you can borrow from later. However, there's a *catch*: you have to pay interest when you borrow against the cash value of your whole life policy. This is because you're borrowing from the insurance company and not from your own money. Also, the insurer chooses the investments so you are limited to their options, which may be conservative. Data shows that the effective return after fees plus insurance costs tends to be much lower than what you can earn with index funds and other alternative investments. In short, getting Term saves you money today, still provides the coverage you need, and allows you to invest the difference you would have spent on the whole life policy in anything you want in your brokerage or IRA.

- Employer perks: Use HSA (Health Savings Account) /FSA (Flexible Savings Accounts) to pay medical bills pre-tax. An HSA is only available if you have a high-deductible health plan, and the money rolls over year after year - you keep it even if you change jobs. An FSA employer-based and is usually "use it or lose it."
  - Tip: If you don't need to tap into your HSA for medical expenses, you can allow this account to grow as an additional investment account. More on this later in Chapter #.

Childcare & Family Needs

- Consider childcare pooling or sharing —trade babysitting with trusted friends/family or split costs for a nanny/babysitter when possible.

- Employer benefits: Some jobs offer dependent care, FSA, backup care benefits or childcare discounts.

- Buy secondhand: clothes, toys, and baby gear can be purchased new or like-new at big savings online and locally at consignment stores.

- Meal prep for kids: Pre-packed snacks at home are up to 70% cheaper than store-bought versions of the same foods.

 *Everyday Hacks*

- Track & review bills monthly: small autopays can hide big leaks.
- Transfer any money that you save to your savings/debt payoff efforts
- Keep your budget for groceries, gas, and entertainment in cash envelopes so you can keep track of exactly how much you spend in real time.
- Ask Yourself: Is this a need or a want? Sometimes "essential" spending is inflated by convenience.
- Success Tip: Build in "fun money" to avoid budget burnout.

Step 3: Acknowledge Your Spending Red Flags

We can't clearly navigate a path forward if we don't understand what got us to where we are. Spend some time sitting with your budget. It's important to reflect on your spending habits and triggers so that you can recognize the situations that led you to make poor financial decisions and also identify the things that motivate you to make good financial decisions. The point of this exercise isn't to shine a light on the imperfections, but rather to identify the areas for improvement so that we can tailor a plan for success. Refer back to the Monthly Spending Snapshot on pp. 34-36:

- What spending surprised you this month? Highlight these entries in *yellow*
- Where can you cut back or reallocate funds? Highlight these entries in ***orange***
- Identify patterns and triggers:
  - Do you notice any impulse purchases? What triggered these purchases? (stress, boredom, etc.) Write these triggers in the "notes" sections of the budget categories.
  - Do you notice any unexpected costs (overdraft fees, incorrect charges, subscriptions you forgot about)? Highlight these entries in **blue**.

- One financial goal for next month:

  ____

  ____

  ____

If your monthly template is looking like a neon explosion, don't worry!

For your *yellow* entries:

- Pick one spending habit to improve this month. Repeat, repeat, repeat.

For the ***orange*** entries:

- Pick one spending area to cut. Repeat, repeat, repeat.

For your patterns and triggers:

- When you notice one of your triggers happening (boredom, stress, etc.) make a conscious decision to substitute spending with an activity that you enjoy and that makes you feel good about yourself (i.e., exercise, catching up on a show or book, checking out a free activity in your area, etc.)

For your ***blue*** entries:

- Dispute any transactions that are errors.
- As your bank to waive your overdraft fee as a one-time courtesy. and check whether they offer overdraft spending protection that will block any transaction that you don't have the money to cover.

- Call the company that charged you a subscription and explain that you did not realize you were still being charged for a service you no longer utilize and ask them to reverse the charge.

Success Tip: Use an app or a simple spreadsheet for more precise and detailed tracking.

It's critical to really dig deep to understand what drives your spending behaviors. Is it insecurity? A "YOLO" mentality? Trying to keep up with the Joneses on social media? Depression? The reality is that most people are struggling and can't afford their lifestyle. Most people don't even know what their biggest bank account drainers are, and even if they do, they don't have the discipline or confidence to live humbly within their means.

I learned this lesson when I realized that my prized possession at the time—my Black sports car —was too much car for my budget! I foolishly traded my perfectly good and fully paid off economy car that was gifted to me by my parents for a high-interest car note because I thought debt was normal and I deserved to drive something nice! It felt good to have a fancy car that got me attention, but it felt even worse privately struggling to balance paying the car note with affording my essential expenses like rent and food. I didn't realize it at the time, but this was the origin of my financial story. I realized that I could make do with taking the train or borrow my mom's car if I needed to (thanks, Barbara!). I sold my car and never looked back. Freeing up this money in my budget allowed me to have money for essentials, save for emergencies, and not feel stressed about managing my finances. After this, I started to look for other areas where I could scale back to make room for financial abundance.

Are you under water on your car note? Up to your eyeballs in Buy Now, Pay later payments for trips and clothes and other non-essentials so that you can impress other people or temporarily boost your spirits? I'm definitely not judging but, as your accountability partner and person who has been there, I am telling you that this is the separator for building wealth. When you find a way to live below your means and stay down until you come up, your progress will take off in ways you didn't think were possible.

Step 4: Attack the Debt

Any progress that you can make towards paying off debt matters, but having a strategic plan can save you time, money, and energy. The debt snowball and debt avalanche methods are two tried and true approaches to crushing debt without complicating the process. Understanding the difference between these two methods is key to choosing the right payoff strategy that fits both your mindset and your money. I will address the snowball method first, because that's the method that worked best for me and typically works best for my clients.

Snowball: Smallest to largest balance (regardless of interest rate).

How it works: You pay off your debts starting with the smallest balance first, regardless of the interest rate. While making minimum payments on all other debts, you put any extra money toward the smallest one. Once that's gone, you move on to the next smallest—like rolling a snowball that slowly builds momentum as it grows.

✅ Pros:

- Quick wins build motivation: You see results fast, which can help you stay emotionally engaged.
- Boosts confidence: Fully paying off an account feels like a win and can build momentum.
- Simple to follow: It's easy to track and encourages consistency.

⚠️ Cons:

- May cost more in interest: Since you aren't prioritizing interest rates, you could pay more over time.

Avalanche: Highest to lowest interest rate.

How it works: You pay off your debts starting with the highest interest rate first, regardless of balance. You make minimum payments on all other debts and throw any extra cash at the most expensive one.

✅ Pros:

- Saves more money: You pay less interest over time.
- Faster total payoff (in many cases): If you stick with it, it's often the quickest route financially.

⚠️ Cons:

- Can feel slower at first: If your highest-interest debt has a large balance, it may take a while to see progress.
- Less emotionally motivating: Some people lose steam without early wins.

🧠 So Which One Should You Use?

- Choose Debt Snowball if: You need quick wins to stay motivated and take consistent action.
- Choose Debt Avalanche if: You're disciplined, math-driven, and want to minimize interest costs.

Personally, when I started my financial wellness journey, my friends and I started a "debt payoff challenge" with a cash prize for whoever could pay off their student loan debt the fastest. I used the snowball method. I'm extremely competitive so I was throwing every extra dollar at my debt—from my employee bonuses to the change between the couch cushions. Seeing the balance get closer and closer to zero gave me an adrenaline rush that I hadn't felt in a long time and made me feel a deep sense of pride in what I was building. The added bonus of accountability partners—who also happened to be my friends that I wanted to see win with money too—encouraged me to go even harder and was exactly the push that I needed to lock into my goal of being debt free. After three short years, I was able to knock out **$37k** of student loans on a $40k salary. Doing this was confirmation that I can conquer any financial goal I set my mind to with the right attitude and fortitude.

Step 5: Adjust As You Grow

So you've built a plan, started attacking your debt, and made some serious progress. You're feeling yourself, AS YOU SHOULD!

But then—life happens.

Your rent goes up. You switch jobs. A surprise car repair wipes out your savings. Or maybe you're doing better than ever and want to level up faster. That's where this crucial step comes in: Adjustment.

In real life, financial plans don't stay frozen in time. They grow with you. Just like your fitness plan changes as you get stronger or your skincare routine shifts with the seasons, your money strategy needs to be flexible, responsive, and realistic.

Let's talk about how (and why) to adjust your financial plan like a pro.

🔄 Why Adjustment Is Part of the Process

You're not failing if you have to change your budget or reset your goals. You're evolving. Here's why it's normal—and necessary—to adjust:

- Life is unpredictable. Emergencies, job changes, family responsibilities, or global events (hello, inflation/pandemic) can throw your plans off.

- You grow. Your income might increase. Your values might shift. What mattered to you financially a year ago might not be a priority today.

- Clarity comes with action. Sometimes, you don't know what's working until you've tried it. Adjustments help refine your strategy.

🔍 **Signs It's Time to Adjust Your Plan**

You don't need a financial crisis to make a change. Here are signs your plan may need tweaking:

- You're consistently overspending in certain categories.

- Your debt payoff is slower (or faster) than expected.

- Your emergency fund has taken a hit.

- Your goals or priorities have changed.

- You've had a major life event: new job, relocation, baby, marriage, personal tragedy, or health emergency.

- You feel stressed, restricted, or disconnected from your current budget.

🛠️ **Adjusting Without Falling Off Track**
Here's how to check in and make smart changes when needed:

Revisit Your Budget Monthly
Treat your budget like a living document. Review it at least once a month—especially after life changes. Are your categories still accurate? Are your savings goals realistic? Make tweaks instead of abandoning the plan.

Reevaluate Your Debt Strategy
Are you still using the debt avalanche or snowball method? Is it working for your current income and mindset? If you've paid off a major loan or increased your income, consider shifting how much you allocate to debt each month. Also consider applying "found" money (bonuses, tax refunds) to your top-priority debt.

Update Your Goals
Your short-term and long-term goals should evolve with you. Finished saving your emergency fund? Cool. Start investing! Paid off a credit card? Shift that money to start a side hustle or to boost a home savings goal!

Track the Wins and Gaps
Keep tabs on what's working (wins) and what's not (gaps). Wins fuel motivation. Gaps are opportunities to improve, not shame triggers.

<u>Staying Motivated</u>

- *Keep progress visible*: Color charts, progress bars, or payoff thermometers
- *Celebrate small wins*: Every milestone achieved deserves a low-cost reward
- *Break the debt into "mini goals"*: Focus on the next balance, not the total
- *Replace spending dopamine*: Workouts, journaling, walks, or learning
- *Remember your "why"*: Less stress, freedom, options, peace

Here are fun and budget-friendly ways to celebrate your wins and stay motivated while paying off large debt. Use web searches and Event apps to research events like these near you:

- *Free community events*: Outdoor movies, festivals, concerts
- *At-home experiences*: Game nights, themed dinners, spa days, movie marathons
- *Nature*: Parks, hikes, beach days, long walks with podcasts
- *Self-improvement*: Learn something new from friends or YouTube (gardening, a new language, hobby, etc.)
- Low-cost treats: Coffee dates, dessert outings, happy-hour specials

Remember: Fun doesn't disappear on a budget — it just gets more intentional.

Stay Emotionally Honest

Adjusting your plan isn't just about numbers—it's about mindset. Be real with yourself. Are you bored with your plan? Burnt out? Tempted to splurge? Financial health includes emotional balance, not just mental discipline.

Real-Life Example: The Pivot

When I worked in car rental I made $40k per year and used the debt snowball method to pay down debt on my tight budget. After landing a new job in pharmaceutical sales, my income jumped by $35K. Instead of sticking rigidly to my old plan, I:

- Increased my emergency fund goal from $1K to $5K
- Reallocated bulk of extra cash toward debt and 401k
- Added a bit more "fun" money to help me stay motivated along the way

Result? I felt more aligned, more balanced, and still on track for debt freedom—with breathing room.

Adjusting doesn't mean starting over or giving up. It means leveling up. Adjusting your plan keeps you engaged, empowered, and in control. Whether you're making micro-changes or massive shifts, the key is to stay honest, flexible, and intentional.

Your plan is a tool—not a prison. It should grow with your life, your values, and your vision.

🔑 Money Moves for the "Adjust" Step

- Schedule a monthly "Money Date" to review and revise your budget.
- Revisit your debt strategy and goal deadlines quarterly.
- Give yourself permission to shift priorities without guilt.
- Ask: Is this plan serving who I am today —not just who I was when I started?

Final Word: Pivot with Power
Your financial journey isn't always uphill. It zigzags, detours, and loops back sometimes. So, when it's time to adjust, don't see it as a setback. You're in charge of your money—and that means having the courage to pivot and adapt when necessary. Breaking up with broke isn't about being perfect. It's about staying in the game and being intentional.

🔍 CHECK-IN: What's Changed Since You Started?

Use this checklist to reflect, realign, and reset your money goals. Mark any that apply:

□ New job or income change

□ Unexpected expense/emergency

□ Big purchase (car, home, etc.)

□ Paid off a debt

□Life milestone (relocation, marriage, baby, breakup, etc.)

□ Change in goals or priorities

□ Feeling overwhelmed or unmotivated

Other changes: ______________________________

____

____

📊 CURRENT STATUS SNAPSHOT

Monthly Income (after taxes): $__________

Total Debt Remaining: $__________

Emergency Fund Balance: $__________

Current Net Worth: $__________

Credit Score: __________

🎯 WHAT'S WORKING?

List 2–3 things in your plan that feel effective or empowering:

1.
2.
3.

⚠️ WHAT NEEDS ADJUSTMENT?

List 2–3 areas where your plan feels misaligned or needs an update:

1.
2.
3.

🛠️ACTION PLAN: TIME TO ADJUST

Choose one or more:

□ Update your budget

□ Adjust debt/savings percentages

□ Set new short-term goals

□ Create a new emergency savings target

□ Update your timeline for debt payoff

□ Add/remove subscriptions or spending categories

□ Increase income (side hustle, raise, etc.)

□ Find new motivation and create an environment that aligns with your goals

My specific adjustment(s):________________

____

____

____

____

✨ **AFFIRMATION**

Write a statement to remind yourself this is part of the process, not a failure: "I give myself permission to adjust my financial plan and my environment so they fit the life I'm building, not the one I've outgrown."

You can write your own:___________________

____

____

____

Step 5: Applaud Your Wins

You've done the budgeting. You've made the sacrifices. You've adjusted when life threw you curveballs. And now, you're further than where you started—and that matters.

But here's something too many people skip: celebrating the wins.

We're conditioned to believe that unless we're completely debt-free or hitting six figures, we shouldn't be clapping for ourselves yet. That mindset? It keeps you stuck. The truth is, small wins lead to big breakthroughs, and acknowledging your progress fuels your momentum. The other truth is that even though your wins might feel small compared to what you see on social media, some of the folks you may be comparing yourself to present a shiny lifestyle but are actually drowning or fronting. Remember: you have no idea how someone is doing financially just based on what you can see.

Let's talk about why—and how—you need to applaud your financial wins along the way.

🎉 Why Celebrating Progress Matters

1. It reinforces good habits.
When you recognize your effort, your brain releases dopamine—a feel-good chemical that makes you want to keep going. It's the same principle that keeps people hooked on social media. But in this case, you're hooked on your own success.

2. It makes the journey sustainable.
Let's be real: financial freedom is a marathon, not a sprint. If you never pause to reflect, you'll burn out. Celebration makes the journey feel human.

3. It rewires your identity.
You're not just "trying to get out of debt" anymore. You're someone who manages money well, hits goals, and celebrates growth. That mental shift changes everything.

🏆 What Counts as a Win?

You don't need to wait until you're 100% debt-free to celebrate. Here are some examples of what's worth applauding:

- Saying "no" to a large purchase that didn't align with your goals
- Paying off a credit card or a loan
- Hitting a milestone like saving $500 or reaching a 700 credit score
- Sticking to your budget three months in a row
- Increasing your income with a raise or side hustle

💡 If it took effort, discipline, patience, or courage—it's a win!

👏 Applauding Without Undoing Your Progress

Celebrating doesn't mean blowing your budget. It means rewarding yourself in ways that feel good and aligned.

Ideas for budget-conscious celebrations:

- Take yourself on a free or low-cost self-care day (Pilates class, movies, picnic, coffee/ ice cream, your favorite meal)
- Buy a small gift that reminds you of your progress (a candle, mug, shirt)
- Post your win in a money accountability group, on social media, or journal it
- Plan a "treat yourself" category in your budget (yes, celebration can be built in!)

Want to splurge? I get it. But first, set a milestone rule: For example, "When I pay off $6,000 in debt, I'll take a $300 weekend trip." **Be ambitious and push yourself!**

This gives you something exciting to look forward to without sabotaging your progress.

✍ **Make Applauding a Practice**

The most successful people don't wait until the finish line to feel proud. They celebrate every step along the way.

Here's how to make it part of your regular money routine:

- At the end of each month, write down one win (big or small). Writing down your achievements is important, because it boosts confidence, helps with reflection, and can even motivate future success by creating a habit of recognizing wins.
- At the end of each quarter, choose a small way to celebrate.
- Keep a "WINS" list in your phone, planner, or budget app.
- Say it out loud: "I'm proud of myself for ____________."

Real-Life Win: **From Shame to Reward**

When I started my financial journey, I had to shift my mindset around spending. I was used to feeling shame whenever I thought about buying non-essentials, because in the past, my bad habit of overspending was holding me back from reaching my financial goals.

To keep myself motivated, I would give myself a prize to reward my progress or mark a financial milestone. Every time I paid off a large credit card debt, I rewarded myself with a pair of sneakers or a fun night out. It would remind me that the very reason I was doing this process was to be able to afford to enjoy myself and live life on my own terms.

✨ **Final Word: You Deserve the Applause**
You're not just breaking up with broke—you're building something new. And every decision you've made to change your story deserves recognition.

So, take a moment. Clap for yourself. Brag a little. Reflect on how far you've come—even if you're not "there" yet.

You didn't wait until you were perfect. You started. You showed up. You adjusted. And now, it's time to applaud.

Next Steps: Reflect, Celebrate, Repeat.
The journey is far from over—but you're no longer broke. You're building wealth, confidence, and a life on your terms.

Use this page to recognize your financial victories and reward your hard work in meaningful, budget-friendly ways.

🏆 WIN TRACKER

Big or small, a win is a win. List your victories here to stay motivated and remind yourself that you're breaking up with broke every day.

Date	My Financial Win	How It Felt / What I Learned
____	______________________	______________________
____	______________________	______________________
____	______________________	______________________
____	______________________	______________________
____	______________________	______________________

🎉 MONTHLY CELEBRATION LOG

Celebrate each month's progress in a way that fuels your momentum (not your debt). Reflect, reward, and reset.

Month	What I'm Proud Of This Month	How I Celebrated / Plan to Celebrate
Jan.	______________________	______________________
Feb.	______________________	______________________
March	______________________	______________________
April	______________________	______________________
May	______________________	______________________
June	______________________	______________________
July	______________________	______________________
Aug.	______________________	______________________
Sept.	______________________	______________________
Oct.	______________________	______________________
Nov.	______________________	______________________
Dec.	______________________	______________________

✨ AFFIRMATION CORNER

Write a few positive statements to remind yourself that you deserve to be celebrated:

“I am proud of my progress, no matter how small. Every step I take brings me closer to financial freedom.”

Write these somewhere where you can read them daily and easily refer to them whenever you need some extra encouragement (on your phone, on a post-it note at your desk, in your bedroom or bathroom):

✨ AFFIRMATION 1

____

____

____

✨ AFFIRMATION 2

____

____

____

✨ AFFIRMATION 3

____

____

____

THE 5-A WAY

1. ANALYZE

2. ACKNOWLEDGE

3. ATTACK

4. ADJUST

5. APPLAUD

The **5-A Way** is your blueprint for breaking up with broke for good. You started with **Analysis**, taking an honest look at your financial picture so you could see exactly where you stand. Then you learned to **Acknowledge** your current reality—both the wins and the mistakes—so you can move forward with clarity, not shame. From there, you **Attacked** your debt with intention, creating a plan to pay it down strategically and consistently. When life threw curveballs, you learned to **Adjust**, making smart pivots without abandoning your goals. And finally, you paused to **Applaud**—celebrating your progress, your new habits, and your growing confidence.

Each "A" builds on the last, turning small steps into lasting change. The **5-A Way** helps you shift from reactive to proactive, from overwhelmed to organized, and from broke to ballin'. Now, you've got the roadmap. The next step is to stay consistent, because mastering your money isn't about perfection; it's about commitment. YOU GOT THIS!

CHAPTER 3

SAVINGS SYSTEMS THAT STICK

Let's get one thing straight: saving money isn't just about discipline—it's about systems. Systems save you from slip-ups, support your financial goals, and most importantly, they help you build a life where you're not one emergency away from a full-on meltdown. In this chapter, we're going to break down the building blocks of smart saving—emergency funds, automation, and sinking funds—so you can finally stop starting over and create a savings system that actually sticks.

Why Saving Feels So Hard—And How to Fix It

If you've ever felt like your money vanishes the second it hits your account or like there's too much month at the end of your money (yes, you read that right), you're not alone. Here's the hard truth: your willpower alone isn't going to save your savings. That's not a character flaw—it's human nature. That's why creating systems is crucial. Systems take emotion and inconsistency out of the equation. They create consistency, clarity, and control. And those three things? They're the enemies of broke.

Let's break down what a solid savings system actually looks like.

SECTION 1
THE EMERGENCY FUND: YOUR FINANCIAL FIRST RESPONDER

An emergency fund is the financial equivalent of a fire extinguisher—you hope you never have to use it but absolutely need to have it ready. It's your first line of defense when life throws punches: car trouble, surprise medical bills, job loss, etc. You might be used to relying on a credit card for emergencies, but this is a big "**no no**." Think about it: if you don't have the money to fund the emergency, you probably won't have the money to pay it off anytime soon either. The longer that balance sits, the more interest you're charged, and the more steps backwards you would be taking away from your goals.

💰 **How Much Should You Have?**

- Starter Emergency Fund:
    - If you're still paying off high-interest debt, start with $1,000-$2,000. This covers small emergencies and keeps you from pulling out the credit card every time life happens. Remember, you may need more if you have dependents.

- Fully Funded Emergency Fund:
    - Once you're out of debt (except your mortgage), aim for at least 6 months of essential living expenses. Think housing, food, insurance, utilities, transportation—not Netflix & brunch.

🛠 What Is It For?

Your emergency fund is for unexpected, necessary, and urgent expenses only. Not birthday dinners. Not vacations. Not the new iPhone or Kendrick concert tickets. Not things you "forgot" to plan for.

Legit uses include:

- Job loss
- Emergency home or car repairs
- Medical emergencies
- Unexpected travel for family crisis

Say it with me: ***If it's not urgent, not unexpected, and not necessary—it's not an emergency***.

💡 **Workbook Prompt**:
List 3 examples of true emergencies you've faced in the past 2 years.

1.

2.

3.

Were you financially prepared for them? If not, what did you do to cover the cost?

Next, write down 3 situations you might face this year that would qualify as emergencies and estimate how much each might cost. For example, is your car on its last leg? Do you have a terminally ill relative that lives in another state? Are you being treated unfairly at work and sense a termination is coming? These are the types of emergencies that we may not always be able to predict, but we can have a plan in place to prepare for them just in case.

1.

2.

3.

🏦 **Where Should You Keep It?**
Keep your emergency fund:

- Out of sight but easy to access
- In a high-yield savings account (HYSA)—so it earns some interest while it sits
- Separate from your other savings so you don't "accidentally" spend it

Don't tie it up in a Certificate of Deposit ("CD"). A CD is a savings account that pays a fixed interest rate on a deposit for a set period of time, or "term." You agree to keep your money in the account for the ***entire*** term, which can range from a few months to several years, in exchange for earning a higher interest rate than a typical savings account. Withdrawing money before the term ends usually results in a penalty.

Don't invest it either. I don't care if your friend just told you about the newest crypto or if you've got a hunch about some stock you read about in the news. Liquidity is king here. If you have to pay a penalty to access money in a pinch, you are hustling backwards.

🔎 **Workbook Prompt**:
Do you currently have a high-yield savings account (HYSA)?

- Yes
    - It is held at: ____________________
    - The current APY is _____________
        - Annual Percentage Yield ("APY") is the amount of interest an account will earn in one year. You can find this information on your account statement or advertised on the bank or institution's website.

- No, but I will open one by: _______ (date)
    - Research 1–2 options this week and look for:
        - zero or low minimum balance requirements
        - no fees (check for monthly maintenance fees, withdrawal or transfer fees, and paper statement fees)
        - high interest rates (remember, this is interest *your* money earns while it sits, not interest you are paying out). Some banks offer a high promotional introductory rate that lasts for a limited time before dropping. This rate still beats what you would be earning from a regular savings account.

- Accessibility and convenience (customer service, familiarity with the institution's reputation)
- Your deposits should be federally insured, typically up to $250,000. Banks and the government get impacted by emergencies too and you want to make sure your money is protected.

SECTION 2
AUTOMATE YOUR FINANCES TO PROTECT YOURSELF FROM...YOURSELF

Here's a universal money truth: if you wait until the end of the month to save "whatever's left," you'll end up saving nothing. It's not entirely your fault. It is how we are wired as humans.

🔄 The Pay-Yourself-First Principle

Treat savings like a bill you have to pay on your monthly budget. That means transferring money from your checking account to your savings every time you get paid until you reach your savings goal and then stop saving money. Whether it's $25 or $250, the key is consistency.

🚨 Why Automation Works:

- No decisions = no delays. You don't have to think about it every time.
- It eliminates temptation. Money that's moved is money you're not spending.

- It builds habits without effort. Set it and forget it—but watch it grow!

🛠 **How to Set It Up:**

- Open a separate HYSA if you haven't already. Pick which ever one has a competitive interest rate and requires a low balance to keep the account active).
- Set up automatic transfers from your checking to savings on payday.
- Name your savings account something motivating (like "Emergency Fund" or "Freedom Fund").

Pro tip: Most online banks let you nickname your accounts. Naming your savings something meaningful keeps your goals top of mind.

✅ Workbook Prompt:
What amount could you commit to saving automatically every time you get paid—even if it's small?

$_________ per paycheck

Set a calendar reminder to automate it this week.

SECTION 3
SINKING FUNDS: SAVING WITH INTENTION

Not all expenses are emergencies. Some are just predictable but irregular—like holiday gifts, medical bills, weddings and baby showers, end of the year property taxes or annual membership fees. Enter: sinking funds.

What's a Sinking Fund?
A sinking fund is money you set aside in advance for a future expense. It's the opposite of surprise or impulse spending—it's planned, purposeful, and pressure-free.

🏝️ **Common Sinking Fund Categories:**

- Holidays & birthdays
- Baby shower
- Wedding
- Travel
- Car maintenance
- Back-to-school shopping
- Kids sports
- Medical co-pays
- Home repairs
- Annual subscriptions and insurance (homeowner's insurance, property taxes, etc.)

💡 **How to Create One:**
1. Pick your categories. Choose expenses that always show up but still feel like surprises.

2. Estimate the total cost. (Example: You spend $600 on Christmas.)

3. Divide by how many months you have left. (If it's June, you have 6 months to save: $600 ÷ 6 = $100/month.)

4. Automate the savings. Use separate savings buckets or accounts if possible.

Some banks and budgeting apps let you create digital envelopes or sub-accounts so you can keep each sinking fund organized and visible.

🔎**Workbook Prompt**:
What "surprise" expenses pop up every year that you could start sinking funds for?

____
____
____
____

List 3–5 categories and how much you typically spend on each per year:

Category	Estimated Annual Cost	Number of months to Save	Monthly Amount
Christmas	$600	6	$100

Set a reminder to automate savings for each of these. Here's a simple, layered approach to build a system that sticks:

1. Start your emergency fund—aim for $1,000–$2,000 ASAP.

2. Automate saving every paycheck—even if it's just $25.

3. Set up your sinking funds—plan for the predictable.

4. Build your full emergency fund—6 months over time.

Final Thoughts: Saving Isn't Optional—It's Oxygen

You don't rise to the level of your goals—you fall to the level of your systems. Saving isn't just something you "try to do"—it's something you design a system for. When your money has a job and a destination, it's much harder to waste. So, build a system that supports the life you want, and put it on autopilot. Because the truth is, the best way to break up with broke… is to save like your life depends on it (because it does!).

Building wealth isn't just about how much you make—it's about how much you keep and where that money goes. In this chapter, you learned how to create savings systems that actually stick - not short-lived challenges, but sustainable habits that move you closer to your goals.

You explored the power of paying yourself first, automating your savings, and assigning every dollar a purpose. You learned how to break your savings into meaningful buckets—like emergencies, goals, and freedom funds—so you can save intentionally instead of randomly.

Most importantly, you discovered that saving doesn't have to mean restriction. It's about freedom—knowing you have options, security, and a plan when life happens. Whether your goal is to build a three-month cushion, handle emergencies with peace of mind, take your bucket-list vacation without having to stress about credit card interest, or finally stop living check to check, your system will keep you consistent even when motivation fades.

Your money works best when it has direction—and now, so do you.

CHAPTER 4

CREDIT CONFIDENCE

Credit. That one word can spark a range of emotions from pride to panic. For some, it represents wealth—the ability to buy a house, a car, or even qualify for a job. For others, it's a scarlet letter symbolizing years of missteps. Credit doesn't have to be confusing or scary—it's simply a snapshot of how well you manage borrowed money. But for too many people, that snapshot tells an uncomfortable story: one shaped by late starts, misinformation, or financial habits we were never taught. *Credit Confidence* is about changing that narrative.

In this chapter, you'll learn how to stop fearing your credit score and start understanding it. You'll uncover the key factors that make up your score, what lenders really look for, and how to use credit strategically—not emotionally or impulsively.

Whether you're rebuilding after past mistakes, just starting to establish credit, or aiming to reach that coveted 700+ range, this section will give you the roadmap you need. Confidence comes from clarity - and by the end of this chapter, you'll know exactly how to take control of your credit story and use it to build the life you deserve.

Before you can improve your credit, you need to understand what shapes it. Let's start with one of the most misunderstood parts of personal finance: your credit score. For many people, it's this mysterious three-digit number that seems to have way too much power over your life—determining whether you get approved for an apartment, how much you pay for a car, or even if you qualify for that dream home. But here's the truth: your credit score isn't here to control you—it's here to measure your reliability. And when you understand it, you can take that control back.

At the heart of your credit story is something called the FICO score: a number ranging from 300 to 850 that reflects how reliably you handle borrowed money.

What's in a FICO Score?

Your FICO score—the most widely used credit score—is made up of five key components:

1. **Payment History** (**35% of your score**)
This is your track record of paying bills on time. Just one late payment can cause your score to drop significantly.

2. **Amounts Owed** (**30% of your score**)
This is how much debt you owe, particularly on credit cards, compared to your credit limit. This is called credit utilization — and keeping it low (ideally

under 10%) can boost your score.

3. **Length of Credit History (15% of your score)**
The longer you've had credit, the better—especially if it's been managed well.

4. **Credit Mix (10% of your score)**
Having different types of credit—like a student loan, car loan, and a mortgage—can help, but it's not worth chasing if it's not part of your natural financial journey.

5. **New Credit (10% of your score)**
Opening a lot of new accounts or hard inquiries in a short period can hurt your score because it can signal financial desperation.

SECTION 1
KNOW YOUR SCORE

Go online and access your free credit report from at least one bureau. Use this space to record what you find.

Credit Bureau	Score	Notes/Red Flags (Errors, Late Payments, etc.)
Equifax		
Experian		
TransUnion		

Reflection: Do any of these numbers surprise you?

Why I Discourage Credit Card Use

Here's the truth: credit cards are a trap for most people. They're marketed as a tool for building credit, earning rewards, and gaining flexibility. But for too many people, they lead to overspending, debt cycles, stress, and huge interest payments. The root problem isn't just the card — it's the habit: spending money you don't have.

Let's be honest. If your credit card balance rolls over from month to month, the rewards aren't worth the interest. If that airline mile just cost you $84 in finance charges, the math is not mathing.

The real flex? Living below your means and building your financial foundation on cash flow—not credit. When you spend cash, there's an emotional friction that simply doesn't exist with swiping a card. Handing over physical bills forces you to literally watch your money leave your hands, and that creates a moment of pause—a sting that makes you more mindful and aware of what you are giving up. Unlike digital transactions, which feel abstract and almost painless, cash spending feels real and finite. That physical connection is powerful because it slows down impulse purchases, makes you weigh the value of what you are buying, and strengthens your awareness of your financial choices. It's that friction that turns spending into a conscious act instead of an automatic one.

Credit Card Check-Up

List any credit cards you currently have. Be honest — this is just for you.

Card Name	Limit	Current Balance	Interest Rate	Status (Active, Inactive or Closed)

Do any of these cards carry a balance from month to month?

□ Yes

□ No

Are you using credit cards for emergencies, to be able to go into an airport lounge, or rewards? Be honest with yourself. I recommend closing all but **one** credit card. Why? The goal of this process is to simplify your finances, reduce temptation, and build positive habits. The rules:

- Keep a recurring subscription on it to keep it active (something like a $9.99 music subscription that is cheap and easy to track).
- Only use it on the rare occasion you are booking something like a hotel, flight or rental car that can't practically be booked in person with cash or requires a card on file.
- Only use your credit card if you have the cash on hand to pay for the expense in full when you make the purchase.

SECTION 2
USE CREDIT SPARINGLY & CAUTIOUSLY

Strategy to Build (and Rebuild) Credit

Whether you're starting from scratch or bouncing back from damage, here's how to build credit with confidence and without falling back into debt:

1. ALWAYS Pay everything on time and IN FULL

2. Keep utilization low.

If you must use a credit card, pay it off in full each month by the due date, and keep your usage under 10% of your limit at all times.

3. Use a secured credit card (carefully).

If your credit is limited or poor, a secured card (where you provide a cash deposit as collateral) can help you build payment history. Use it for one small recurring bill and pay it off monthly.

4. Consider closing old inactive accounts with annual fees

Length of credit history matters. If you have old cards you no longer use, you can keep them open if there are no annual fees. However, if you are being charged a fee for any of these cards that you don't use, you should close them.

5. Avoid credit traps:

- NEVER co-sign for others.
- NEVER open a store card just to get a shopping discount.
- NEVER take out cash advances.

6. Avoid "Buy Now pay Later":

Companies make billions of dollars by disguising debt as convenience. Don't commit your future income before you even have it. This can pile up quickly, leaving you with "mini debts" that will eat away at your cash flow and make it harder to stay on budget. Buy Now, Pay Later also encourages overspending because it tricks your brain into focusing on the small installment instead of the full cost. On top of that, missed payments can hit your credit score and come with fees that further drain your cash flow.

Use this checklist to commit to healthy credit-building habits:

✅ I will pay all bills on time.

✅ I will keep my credit utilization under 10%.

✅ I will avoid applying for new credit.

✅ I will close old accounts if they have fees or enable my overspending.

✅ I will check my credit reports at least once a year.

✅ I will protect my identity with strong passwords and freeze my credit if needed.

Which of these steps do you need to start today? Circle 1–2 to focus on this week.

SECTION 3
PROTECT YOUR PROGRESS

Monitoring and Protecting Your Credit

You can't fix what you don't see. And you definitely don't want to be blindsided by fraud. Here's how to stay on top of your credit health:

- Check your credit reports at least once a year. You're entitled to a free report from each bureau (Equifax, Experian, and TransUnion). Pro tip: rotate checking each bureau every four months, so you're monitoring year-round without paying for extras.

Review for errors because mistakes happen. Look for: accounts you don't recognize, incorrect balances or payment statuses, duplicate accounts, or collections that should be removed. Use free monitoring tools like Credit Karma or Experian to stay alert to changes in your score. If you find something wrong, dispute it directly with the bureau. It's free, and they're legally required to investigate.

- Set fraud alerts. These tell lenders to verify your identity before issuing credit.
- If you've experienced identity theft, lost your wallet, or want extra protection, consider a credit freeze with the bureaus to prevent identity thieves from opening new accounts in your name. It's free and reversible.

The Myth of Credit Consolidation

A word of caution: ***Don't confuse movement with progress***.

Many people get excited about debt consolidation—rolling all their debt into one loan or transferring balances to a new credit card. It sounds like a fresh start, but it's often just a bandage on a deeper wound. The logic is simple: consolidation doesn't fix ***why*** you're in debt. If you haven't addressed the core issue—spending more than you make — you'll end up in the same place, just with different account numbers. It's like bailing water out of a sinking boat without patching the hole. Instead, focus on building your financial future on cash flow, not credit limits, and practice spending money you already have instead of money you hope to have later.

Credit Is a Tool — Not a Trophy

Credit is important, but it's not everything. You don't need an 850 score to live a wealthy, financially free life. You need good habits, intentional money decisions, and a plan. In this journey, we're not chasing perfect scores. We're building financial peace. That means control, confidence, and clarity — with or without a credit card.

- Understand your FICO score: focus on payment history and low credit usage.
- Avoid unnecessary reliance on credit cards; they often lead to overspending.
- Build credit through responsible habits, not shortcuts.
- Monitor and protect your credit

Building credit confidence means taking control of the factors that shape your financial reputation. In this chapter, you learned how your FICO score reflects 5 key behaviors—payment history, amounts owed, length of credit history, credit mix, and new credit—and how each can work for or against you. You explored practical strategies to strengthen your score, from paying bills early and keeping balances low to avoid credit traps.

Credit confidence isn't about chasing perfection; it's about creating consistency. By applying these principles, you'll move from feeling anxious about your credit report to feeling empowered by it.

Remember:

Step 1: Know your score so you're always clear about where you stand

Step 2: Use credit cards sparingly and cautiously. Do not swipe now and think later.

Step 3: Protect your progress and tune out the noise

CHAPTER 5

INVESTING 101 - BUILDING WEALTH LIKE A PRO

So, you've analyzed your financial situation, **acknowledged** your habits, **attacked** your debt, **adjusted** your plan, **applauded** your progress—and now it's time to **accelerate** your growth by: INVESTING.

Whether you want to retire early, pass down wealth, travel more, buy a home, or simply sleep better knowing your money is working for you, investing is the key. This chapter will walk you through the basics of investing, the accounts that grow your money tax-free or tax-deferred, the order to use them in, and how to build a solid long-term plan—even if you're starting from scratch.

💡 *Why Investing Matters (a.k.a. What Broke Doesn't Want You to Know)*

Saving is essential but, investing is where real wealth is built. Saving puts money aside. Investing puts money to work.

Think of investing like planting seeds. Over time—with enough sunlight (contributions), good soil (your strategy), and patience (not panic-selling)—those seeds turn into fruit-bearing trees. The earlier you start, the bigger the harvest. Also, just like you shouldn't pick fruit before it's ripe, you must not disturb your investments before they have enough time to grow! Let's talk about the magic ingredient (your fertilizer): compound interest.

The Power of Compound Interest

Compound interest is when your money earns money… and then that money earns money… and then that money earns money. Over time, this snowball effect creates serious growth.

For example:

- If you invest $300/month from age 25 to 65 and average a 7% return, you'll have over $760,000.
- Wait until 35 to start? That drops to $370,000.

Tip: Time in the market beats timing the market. Don't wait for the "perfect" time—get in the game early and stay consistent.

SECTION 1
GET SET TO INVEST

Investing Basics: What Am I Actually Buying?

When you invest, you're buying ownership—whether it's a piece of a company through stocks or a share of pooled funds. The stock market is one of the most powerful tools for building long-term wealth. While it comes with great rewards for those who are patient, consistent, and responsible, several factors like economic conditions, corporate scandals, and news events can create volatility and risk.

Responsible and informed investing allows you to put your money to work so it can grow over time with minimal effort from you. In this section, you'll learn what each investment type really represents, how it earns money, and why understanding what you own is key to building lasting wealth.

- ***Stocks***
  - Owning a slice of a company.
  - If the company grows, your investment grows too.
  - Stocks trade on exchanges and their prices move constantly all day, based on supply and demand, company news, and market activity. The price you see—called the market price—changes constantly while the market is open.
  - High risk, high reward.

- ***Bonds***
  - When you buy a bond, you're lending money to a government, city, or company, and in return, they pay you interest over time.
  - Lower risk, lower reward. Good for balance.

ETFs, index funds, and mutual funds are all investment vehicles that pool money from multiple investors, but they differ in structure, trading methods, and management styles.

- ***Mutual Funds***
  - a pool of money collected from many investors to buy a mix of stocks, bonds, or other assets. This translates to easy diversification.
  - A professional manager chooses and manages the investments for everyone in the fund. This comes at a cost since they are using skill to try and beat the market. Beware: higher fees do not mean higher returns!
  - You own a small piece of the overall fund, not individual stocks
  - Priced only once per day and often have minimum investment requirements of at least $500
- ***ETFs (Exchange-Traded Funds)***
  - A bundle of investments (stocks, real estate, gold) that you can buy like a single stock.

  - Instead of buying shares of one company, you can buy shares of thousands of companies at once!
  - Passively managed (usually tracks an index like the S&P 500, which is made up of the 500 largest US Companies) vs. actively managed like a mutual fund. Great for diversification—own pieces of hundreds of companies in one fund.
  - Many ETFs are index funds (more on these next).
  - They trade all day, like a stock.
- ***Index Fund***
  - Instead of a manager picking individual "winning" stocks, an index fund simply buys all (or most) of the companies in a given index and holds them. For example, if you invest in an index fund that tracks the S&P 500, you're investing in 500 of the largest U.S. Companies—like Apple, Microsoft, Amazon, and Google—all at once. If the index goes up, your fund goes up, and vice versa.
  - Can only be bought or sold at the end of the trading day at the net asset value price.
  - Generally have lower expense ratios compared to actively managed mutual funds, making them cost-effective options for investors.

Use the Right Tools: Tax-Advantaged Accounts

You've got multiple buckets you can invest in, but some are better than others because they protect your gains from taxes. Let's walk through the different types and the pros and cons/limits of each.

What Is a 401(k)

A 401(k) is a retirement savings account you get through your job. You put in money from each paycheck, it gets invested, and it grows over time so you have money to use when you stop working.

2026 Contribution Limits

- *Employee contribution limit*: $24,500
- *Total limit* (employee + employer): $72,000.

Why It's So Valuable

1. *Big Tax Benefits*

- Traditional 401(k): You add money before taxes, lowering your taxable income today.
- Roth 401(k) (*not offered by all employers): You pay taxes now, and your money grows tax-free forever.

2. *Employer Match = Free Money*

If your job matches your contributions, any amount they add is **free money** and guaranteed returns you can't get anywhere else.

3. *Automatic Investing*

Your money is automatically invested into diversified funds, so it grows without you having to pick stocks or manage it yourself.

4. *Compounding Growth*
Your contributions earn money, and those earnings earn more money. Over decades, even small contributions can grow into hundreds of thousands of dollars.

5. *High Contribution Limits*
You can put in much more each year than regular retirement accounts allow, helping you build wealth faster.

6. *Harder to Accidentally Spend*
Automatic paycheck contributions force you to save consistently.

Bottom Line
A 401(k) is one of the fastest, easiest, and most tax-efficient ways to build long-term wealth—especially if your employer matches your contributions.

What Is an IRA? ⭐

An IRA (Individual Retirement Account) is a retirement account you open on your own (not through your job). You put in money → it gets invested → it grows for your future. It's one of the easiest ways for anyone to start building retirement wealth.

Contribution Limits for 2026

- Standard annual limit (Traditional & Roth IRAs): $7,500.

Why an IRA Matters

1. Big Tax Benefits
There are two types of IRAs:

- *Traditional IRA*:
    - You get a tax deduction now → money grows tax-deferred → pay taxes later.
        - You put money in (up to $7,500)
        - You get a tax break today (tax deductible)
        - Your money grows tax-deferred
        - You pay taxes when you take the money out in retirement
    - *How do I fund my traditional IRA?*
        - **Cash contributions**: Deposit money from your bank account (earned income only).
        - **Roll over an old 401(k)**: Move retirement money from a previous job into an IRA (no taxes if done correctly)
        - **Spousal IRA**: A working spouse can fund an IRA for a non-working spouse.
        - **Transfer from an existing IRA**: (for example, moving your money from one brokerage's IRA over to a different brokerage company's IRA) (note: this is not a contribution, it's consolidation).

- Roth IRA
    - A retirement account that you can open on your own (not tied to a job) where you put in after-tax money now so you can take it out tax-free later. You pay taxes today → your money grows → you withdraw in retirement with no taxes owed.

- Eligibility to contribute is based on your income ($153,000 for single filers and $252,000 for married couples)
  - 2026 Contribution Limits
    - Base limit: $7,500 if you're under age 50.

- You pay taxes now → money grows tax-free.
  - You put money in after taxes (no tax break today) up to $7,500
  - Your money grows tax-free
  - You pay zero taxes when you withdraw in retirement

- How do I fund my ROTH IRA?
  - **Earned Income**: Contributions must come from your own taxable compensation.
  - **401(k) Rollover**: You can roll over funds from a previous employer's 401(k) into a Roth IRA.
  - **Roth Conversion**: You can move money from a traditional IRA or 401(k) into a Roth IRA. You will likely have to pay income tax on the amount you convert.
  - **In-Kind Transfers**: You can move existing investments, such as stocks, from another IRA or 401(k) into your Roth IRA without selling them first

Whether you use a Roth or Traditional IRA, you get major tax advantages you don't get in a traditional savings or retirement account.

2. Automatic Long-Term Investing
Your IRA money can be invested in things like index funds, and it grows while you work. More seasoned investors can also select whatever individual stocks they would like to invest in.

3. Compounding Growth
The earlier you invest, the more time your money has to grow. Small monthly deposits can turn into large, long-term gains.

4. You Control It, Not Your Employer
You can open an IRA with any brokerage instead of being tied to your employer's preferred platform.

5. Great for Beginners
IRAs have smaller limits than 401(k)s, but they're perfect if you:

- Don't have a job that offers a 401(k)
- Want extra retirement savings beyond your job plan

Bottom Line
An IRA is a simple, flexible, tax-advantaged retirement account anyone can open. It's one of the easiest ways to start investing and building wealth early.

What Is a 529 Plan? ⭐
A 529 plan is a special savings account for education costs.

- You put in money → it gets invested → it grows tax-free → and you can use it for school expenses without paying taxes. It's the most powerful way to save for a child's future education.

- You can name *anyone* as a beneficiary — a relative, a friend, even yourself.
- There are no income restrictions on either you, as the contributor, or the beneficiary. There is also no limit to the number of plans you set up.
- The IRS does not impose a strict yearly cap on how much you can contribute. You just can't exceed "the amount necessary" to provide for the qualified education expenses of the beneficiary

Why a 529 Is So Valuable

1. *Tax-Free Growth*

Your money grows tax-free as it's invested over time. Similar to a Roth: no taxes on the growth when you use it for education.

2. *Tax-Free Withdrawals (for Education)*

When the money is used for approved costs—tuition, books, laptops, and even some apprenticeships—you pay zero taxes.

3. *High Contribution Limits*

Great for long-term planning. You can contribute much more than you can into an IRA or HSA.

4. *Anyone Can Contribute*

Parents, grandparents, family, friends — anyone can add money to grow the account faster.

5. *More Than College Tuition*

529s can also pay for:

- College expenses (books, housing, etc.)

- Trade school
- K–12 tuition (private school)
- Online education programs
- Some apprenticeships
- Special needs
- Even student loan repayment (up to limits)

6. You Stay in Control
The account owner (usually the parent) controls the money — not the child. You decide when and how it's used.

7. You Can Change the Beneficiary
If the first child doesn't use all the money, you can switch it to:
- Another child
- Yourself
- A spouse
- Even a grandchild

No penalties when switching.

Bottom Line
A 529 plan is the best tax-advantaged way to save for education. Your money grows tax-free, can be used for many education expenses, and gives you long-term flexibility for your family's future.

What Is an HSA?⭐
An HSA is a special savings and investment account for medical expenses. You put in pre-tax money → it grows tax-free → and you can use it anytime, without paying taxes, to pay for qualified health costs. It's one of the most powerful and flexible accounts in all of personal finance.

2026 HSA Contribution Limits

- Self-coverage: $4,400 total contribution limit.
- Family coverage: $8,750 total contribution limit.

Why an HSA Is So Valuable

1. *Triple Tax Benefit* (Best in Finance)

An HSA gives you three tax advantages:

- Tax-free contributions (lowers your taxable income)
- Tax-free growth when invested
- Tax-free withdrawals for medical expenses

No other account gives all three.

2. *Your Money Rolls Over Forever*

Unlike an Flexible Spending Account (more on these in the next section), you *never* lose your money. It stays with you year after year, even if you change jobs or insurance.

3. *Acts Like a Medical Retirement Account*

You can invest your HSA money in index funds. Let it grow for years, then use it tax-free later for:

- Doctor visits
- Prescriptions
- Dental
- Vision
- Hospital bills
- And much more

4. Flexible After Age 65

After 65, you can take money out for ***anything*** (not just medical costs), and it's taxed like a normal retirement account—similar to a Traditional IRA. Medical withdrawals stay tax-free at any age.

5. *Can Be a Wealth-Building Tool*
Many people pay current medical costs out-of-pocket and let their HSA grow untouched. This turns the HSA into a stealth retirement account with unmatched tax benefits.

Bottom Line
An HSA gives you unmatched tax benefits, permanent rollover, and long-term growth. It's one of the smartest accounts to use for current medical costs and for building future wealth.

What Is an FSA?⭐
An FSA is a workplace account that lets you set aside pre-tax money to pay for medical or childcare expenses you know expect to have during the year. You save on taxes, but you must use the money within the plan's rules.

Different Types of FSAs

- *Healthcare FSA*: For medical expenses
- *Dependent Care FSA*: For childcare costs
- *Limited Purpose FSA*: For dental & vision only (usually paired with an HSA)

2026 FSA Contribution Limits

- **Health Care FSA**:
  - Annual contribution limit: $3,400 for plan years beginning January 1, 2026.

  - *Carryover* (if your plan allows): Up to $680 of unused funds can roll over to the next plan year (up from $660).

- **Dependent Care FSA (DCFSA)**:
  - *Maximum per household*: $7,500 (up from $5,000).
  - *If married filing separately*: $3,750 per individual.

Why an FSA Matters

1. *Saves You Money on Taxes*

Money goes in before taxes, lowering your taxable income. You're using "discounted dollars" to pay for everyday medical or childcare costs.

2. *Great for Predictable Expenses*

FSAs are best when you know you'll spend money on things like:

- Copays & prescriptions
- Glasses/contacts
- Dental work
- Childcare (Dependent Care FSA)
- Therapy & mental health
- Over-the-counter medicine

3. Money Usually Must Be Used That Year

FSAs follow use-it-or-lose-it rules. Some jobs allow a small rollover (like $600+) or a grace period to use leftover funds. But generally, you should spend what you set aside in the year you save the money.

4. *Comes Through Your Employer*

You can only get an FSA if your job offers one, and you can't keep it if you leave that employer.

Bottom Line

An FSA helps you save money on medical or childcare costs by letting you use pre-tax dollars, but you must plan carefully because the money typically must be used within the year. It's great for predictable expenses, but less flexible than an HSA.

SECTION 2
GET SET TO INVEST

How to Set These Up

- ***401(k)***
  - Usually offered through your employer. Contact HR or log into your benefits portal.
  - Choose a contribution amount and pick your investments (usually from a list of mutual funds or target-date funds).
- ***Roth IRA / Traditional IRA / Brokerage Account***
  - Can be opened on your own through a brokerage (choose which one is most convenient or matches your personal preferences).

To set up your account:

1. Go to the website of the brokerage.
2. Choose the account type (Roth IRA, Traditional IRA, or Brokerage).
3. Provide your info, link your bank, and fund the account.
4. Pick your investments (keep reading!)

SECTION 3
PICK YOUR INVESTMENTS LIKE A PRO

What Should You Invest In?

You don't need to be the next Warren Buffett to win with investing. Start with low-cost index funds. An index fund is a type of fund designed to copy the performance of a specific market index like the S&P 500 or Dow Jones. Because no fund manager is constantly buying and selling to "beat the market," fees are usually much lower than actively managed funds. They have built in diversification so one purchase gets you access to dozens or hundreds of companies. In short, an index fund is a low-cost, hands-off way to own a big piece of the stock market.

Examples of Low-Cost Index Funds:

- VTI (Vanguard Total Stock Market ETF)
- VOO (Vanguard S&P 500 ETF)
- FZROX (Fidelity ZERO Total Market Index)
- SCHB (Schwab U.S. Broad Market ETF)

Look for low fees (expense ratio under 0.10%) and broad diversification across different sectors like tech, healthcare and energy.

! DISCLAIMER

While I can share my personal favorites, ***please do not take this as binding financial advice***, because I cannot give that out without knowing anything about your personal situation and circumstances. **Always do your own research first before investing your money and make sure you understand the risks**.

Avoid These Common Mistakes

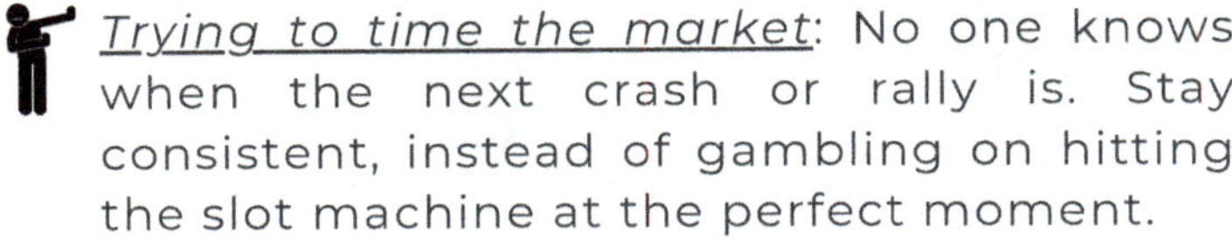

Trying to time the market: No one knows when the next crash or rally is. Stay consistent, instead of gambling on hitting the slot machine at the perfect moment.

Panic selling: The market will dip. But history has shown it has only gone up over time. Stick to your long-term plan.

Over-checking your portfolio: Check it quarterly, not daily. There will be ups and downs and if you are overdoing it with the check-ins, your blood pressure might be up and down too.

Ignoring fees: High-fee mutual and index funds can eat away your returns. Stick to low-cost index funds with fees under .10%.

Example: If you invested $1,000 a month over a 40-year career, you can expect your portfolio to grow to about $5.8 million. If you paid an advisor a 1% fee—which is standard for the industry you end up with $4.3 million. The one percent fee cost us about $1.5 million, or 25% of our wealth!

Some great funds have fees as low as between .015% and .03%. Every dollar matters!

Final Tips for New Investors

1. Start now—even if it's just $50/month.
2. Automate everything—set up recurring contributions.
3. Diversify—don't put all your eggs in one stock or sector.
4. Be patient—wealth building takes time, not luck.
5. Keep learning—read books, listen to podcasts, follow trusted financial educators.

Final Thoughts

Investing doesn't require a finance degree, fancy tools, or thousands of dollars. It requires consistency, patience, and strategy. You can do this, and your future wealthy self is cheering for you!

Action Step:

Open a Roth IRA ***today*** (or a personal brokerage if you don't meet the Roth eligibility requirements). Fund it with what you can—even if it's $50. Choose a low-fee index fund. Then, commit to a monthly auto-contribution. Your journey to building wealth just leveled up.

CHAPTER 6

LONG-TERM MONEY MOVES

Build the Vision. Fund the Dream. Stay the Course.

Let's be real—getting out of debt is great, but that's just the beginning. The real flex? Building the kind of life you don't need to escape from. And not just on social media either (cough cough). That's what long-term money goals are really about.

My desire to be rich didn't start out flashy. At first, I wanted money for one simple reason: to help my mom. Not being able to financially support her at the beginning of her divorce made me feel helpless. I never wanted to feel that way again. Instead, I wanted to be able to be a resource for myself and the people I love.

Then, there was my apartment—Apartment 203. It was in Harlem where I grew up, a few blocks from my mom and her home-cooked meals, and in the middle of my entire friend group. It was freedom, privacy, and peace—everything I felt I had control over at that time. I wanted to be able to afford staying in this sanctuary without having to stress and struggle.

After that, I wanted money for independence. I didn't want my survival or progress to depend on an employer. I

wanted time freedom, options, and control over my days.

From there, my motivation evolved. I wanted to provide for the family I would one day have. I knew that if my financial foundation was solid, I could step into being a husband and father with less stress and more presence and peace.

And yes—eventually, I wanted money to enjoy life. To travel, show up to any concert, game, or event without reservations or restrictions. To live well. A penthouse, some nice cars, watches, jewelry. Fashion without limits—because why not? I knew that once I handled what truly mattered, everything else would follow. And my story is a testament to that.

We're not just here to survive. We're here to build wealth, fund our freedom, and walk in purpose. But that kind of financial future doesn't just fall into your lap—it's built one smart decision at a time, starting with a clear vision and a concrete plan.

If you haven't already figured out your "why" this is the perfect time to start visualizing your long-term goals as we work towards making them reality.

SECTION 1
DEFINE YOUR "WHY FOR WEALTH"

Why Long-Term Goals Matter
When your money has no long-term direction, it gets pulled into short-term distractions. New clothes, last-minute trips, expensive take out every night—it all adds up and leaves you wondering where your paycheck and hard-earned progress went. But when you're aiming for something bigger, you start to think differently about how you earn, spend, save, and invest.

Long-term money goals give your budget purpose and your hustle direction.

Common Long-Term Financial Goals
Here are some common long-term goals for inspiration:

Buy a Home
Whether it's a condo, duplex, or dream house, homeownership can build equity and stability.

- Goal: Save for a down payment (10–20%).

- Pro Goal: Save for a down payment *and* enough to afford a 15-year mortgage which could potentially save you hundreds of thousands of dollars in interest!

Buy or Upgrade a Vehicle
Plan for your next car purchase without debt.
- Goal: Save in advance and avoid long-term auto loans.

- Pro Goal: Buy a modest car in cash so that you can invest the difference and superset your other goals!

Pay for Education

Whether it's your own degree, a child's tuition, or professional certifications, education is an investment in earning potential.

- Goal: Make an extra payment towards your student loan's principal balance (Note: you **must** specify that you want the extra to go to the principal or the lender will automatically apply it to the interest. They want their money FIRST!)

- Pro Goal: Open a 529 Savings Account to start investing early to reap the benefit of compound interest.

Start a Business

Many people dream of becoming their own boss. A solid financial foundation makes it possible.

Retire (or Work Less) Sooner

This isn't just for people over 50. The earlier you plan for financial independence, the more freedom you'll have.

Take a Bucket-List Trip

You can enjoy life *and* be responsible. Set a long-term travel goal and save for it purposefully.

- Goal: Get a side hustle to superset your vacation fund!

SECTION 2
SETTING LONG-TERM MONEY GOALS THAT ACTUALLY HAPPEN

1. Be Specific
Don't just say "I want to retire early." Say, "I want to retire at 55 with $1 million invested and no mortgage."

2. Make It Measurable
Attach a dollar amount and a timeline. If your goal is to buy a house in 5 years, how much do you need to save each year?

3. Break It Into Mini-Milestones
Big goals feel less overwhelming when they're broken into bite-sized steps.

Example:
Goal: Save $25,000 for a house in 5 years
Breakdown: $25,000 ÷ 60 months = ~$417/month

Now it's actionable. Now it's real.

4. Automate It
Treat your long-term goals like a bill. Automate savings and investment contributions so they happen without thinking.

Long-Term Goals vs. Short-Term Sacrifices
Here's the truth: achieving long-term goals does require short-term trade-offs. But they're not punishments—they're priorities. Saying "no" to brunches, luxury cars, or impulse shopping doesn't mean you're

broke or imprisoned. It means you're focused. You're not depriving yourself—you're defining yourself. And every dollar you don't spend on what's easy today becomes a vote for the life you really want tomorrow.

I vividly remember missing **A LOT** over the years while I was focused on getting out of debt. I knew that every event was important to the person inviting me, but if I didn't stick to my boundaries, there would be constant opportunities to derail my progress. Choosing discipline meant saying "no" more often than I wanted to, and that wasn't easy. But those sacrifices created the freedom that allow me to say "yes" today far more than I ever had to say "no." It's not easy to skip events that feel once-in-a-lifetime in the moment—but life is long, and there will be plenty of chances to celebrate. And I promise, those moments feel even better when they're not overshadowed by the weight of debt.

Saying "no" may look like going to a wedding but declining to spends thousands of dollars to be a bridal party member if you just can't afford it. Or, you may take your friend out for lunch instead of spending hundreds at their birthday dinner.

SECTION 3
PROTECTING YOUR PROGRESS

Long-term goals only work if you protect the foundation you're building. That means:

- Sticking to your budget
- Maintaining an emergency fund (so a crisis doesn't wreck your savings plan)
- Avoiding unnecessary debt and lifestyle creep
- Consistently investing
- Reviewing your goals annually

Visualize It: Your Long-Term Goal Map

Grab a notebook, journal, or whiteboard and answer these prompts:

In 10 years, I want to be living (be specific about the location, the type of residence, how is it decorated, what amenities do you have, who are you living with, etc.): ____
____
____
____

I want to be spending my time doing: ____
____
____

My top 3 long-term financial goals are:

- Goal 1: ______________________________
  ____
- Goal 2: ______________________________
  ____
- Goal 3: ______________________________
  ____

I will automate $_______/month toward these goals starting _______________________.

Break Up With Broke, Build Wealth for Life

You've officially broken up with broke. You didn't just read a book. You started a movement. If you've made it this far, pause and take a breath.

Sure, we've talked about debt, credit, budgets, and long-term goals. But you know what this was really about?

- Taking back your power
- Trusting yourself with money
- Breaking cycles and building legacies
- Creating peace—not just in your finances, but in your life

Being broke was never just about income. It was about alignment. And now, you're no longer surviving in financial chaos—you're walking in clarity, purpose, and direction.
Building long-term wealth isn't about luck, inheritance, or hustle culture. It's about clarity, consistency, and commitment. The journey doesn't end here. There will be setbacks. There will be slow months. But now, you've got a system. And more importantly, you've got a standard. From this point on, you're not making financial decisions from desperation. You're making them from discipline. Your role from here is to:

- Keep showing up
- Keep adjusting when life changes
- Keep educating yourself
- Keep talking about money—out loud, boldly, and without shame

When you're clear about what you want, consistent in how you move, and committed to protecting your future—you will reach it. You're not just saving for "someday." You're building the foundation for the life you deserve.

Maybe no one taught you this stuff. Maybe you learned about money through hard lessons like overdraft fees and late notices. Maybe you were handed struggle instead of strategy.

But now? You are the blueprint.

You are the example your younger siblings, your kids, your friends, and your community can look to and say: "If they can do it, I can too." Don't just break up with broke for yourself. Do it for the generation after you. Do it for the people watching you silently. Do it for the version of you who didn't believe this was possible.

CLOSING THOUGHTS

A FINAL WORD FROM ME TO YOU

Thank you for choosing Break Up With Broke and trusting me to guide you on this important journey. Deciding to take control of your money is one of the bravest, most powerful moves you can make. It shows that you believe in yourself—and your future. That commitment to yourself is the foundation of every success you will create. If no one's told you this before:

I'm proud of you. Not because your numbers are perfect, but because you showed up. Remember, this isn't about being perfect—it's about progress, persistence, and purpose. You did the work. You took your power back. You're not behind. You're just getting started. You're not stuck. You're the boss of your life and your finances.

If you ever feel stuck or discouraged, come back to these pages. Revisit your goals. Reflect on your wins. And remind yourself—you are capable, worthy, and absolutely deserving of the life you're building. Stay broken up with broke, keep bossing up, and keep shining your light for others who are ready to follow your lead.

With gratitude and belief in you always,

Alex Finance

Break Up With Broke

You didn't have to do this alone—and you don't have to keep going alone.

Breaking up with broke is more than a personal decision. It's a movement. A community of people just like you—determined to take control of their money, rewrite their stories, and build lives on their own terms.

When you join our community, you get:

- Real talk about money — no judgment, just support
- Accountability partners to cheer you on
- Access to exclusive tips, tools, and challenges
- Inspiring stories from people who started exactly where you are
- Opportunities to celebrate your wins and learn from setbacks

- **Website:** AlexFinanceNYC.com
- **Instagram**: @AlexFinanceNYC
- **Facebook**: AlexFinanceNYC
- **Youtube**: AlexFinanceNYC

Your journey matters — and so does your voice. Come connect. Share your wins. Ask your questions. Lift others up. Because when we grow together, we all win.

Let's do this — together.

Break Up With Broke

www.ingramcontent.com/pod-product-compliance
Lightning Source LLC
Chambersburg PA
CBHW071706210326
41597CB00017B/2351
* 9 7 9 8 9 9 4 3 5 4 2 1 6 *